Many Protestants rightly love Church history but often wonder about wha[...] ween the great theologians of th[...] gence of men such as Martin Lu[...] s the Church simply apostate fo[...] , Iain Wright and Yannick Imber[...] appreciative, though not uncritical, introduction to that missing thousand years, a period that, contra popular Protestant impressions, produced some great and influential Christian thinkers.

CARL TRUEMAN
Professor of Biblical and Religious Studies,
Grove City College, Pennsylvania; Author, *The Wages of Spin*

Iain Wright and Yannick Imbert have given us an enlightening and richly informative study of a much neglected Christian era. To some Christians, the Middle Ages was either a dark age, or an age almost devoid of the gospel. Dr Wright and Dr Imbert have written a fine and richly informative study which will do much to correct these misconceptions. Read and be enriched.

IAN HAMILTON
President, Westminster Seminary, Newcastle, UK;
Author, *The Erosion of Calvinist Orthodoxy*

Evangelicalism, at a popular level, often rejects the Middle Ages as a period of sheer darkness, hardly worth knowing. Iain Wright and Yannick Imbert demonstrate that the medieval period is very much worth knowing. In these pages, we meet a succession of spiritually-minded men from those centuries, some of whom (like Bernard of Clairvaux) the 16th century Reformers would regard as heroes of the faith. I gladly commend this volume as helping us to see the brighter side of what is often looked on as the "dark ages".

NICK NEEDHAM
Tutor in Church History, Highland Theological College, Dingwall;
Author, *2000 Years of Christ's Power*

Reclaiming the "Dark Ages" is refreshing, stimulating, and truly a joy to read! Imbert and Wright call us to recognise and be grateful for the guiding hand of providence in all of Church history, even among some of those family members who, at times, tend to embarrass us! This is a much needed and very welcome book. Bravo! May the Lord give it a broad reach and enthusiastic reception among His children who haven't always valued Church history.

WES BAKER
Missionary, Peru Mission

Reclaiming the "Dark Ages"

How the Gospel Light Shone from 500 to 1500

Iain Wright &
Yannick Imbert

CHRISTIAN
FOCUS

Copyright © Iain Wright and Yannick Imbert 2024

paperback ISBN 978-1-5271-1155-4
ebook ISBN 978-1-5271-1209-4

10 9 8 7 6 5 4 3 2 1

Published in 2024
by
Christian Focus Publications Ltd,
Geanies House, Fearn, Ross-shire,
IV20 1TW, Great Britain.

www.christianfocus.com

Cover design by Rubner Durais

Printed and bound by
Bell & Bain, Glasgow

Acknowledgements

We are grateful for the support and encouragements of the following people, without whom this book would not exist.

Iain—The elders and saints at Covenant Church (Orland Park) for granting me a sabbatical, during which Yannick and I were able to bring this book to completion.

Yannick—Alison Wells who has generously offered to correct my English grammar. Without her efforts, this book might not have reached Christian Focus for a long time!

Anne Norrie, at Christian Focus, for her dedication and wonderful work reading and editing this book.

Contents

Introduction

French Reformed philosopher Jean Brun used to say that humans were the only beings to have a history. He was right. We are not only creatures living in time, as all created beings do, but we also look back to times long past. We write histories. We ponder our personal and collective histories. Whether we are conscious of it or not, we are deeply historical beings, for whom our past is constitutive of our present. This is not only true for our biological roots, but also for everything that makes up human life. Societies are anchored in history, as are our ideas and technologies. This is also true of our faith: its source and truth are dependent on an historical event, the birth, death and resurrection of Christ. Our theology also has a history that we cannot easily dismiss.

During the past fifteen years I (Yannick) have been teaching a brief annual course on the English Reformation. I have been struck, again and again, by the lack of interest in the history of the church—and the history of theology. This lack of interest has many roots. We have sometimes thought of theology as an autonomous task, involving only the individual, their Bible, and a few important theological works that we have read without much thought for their context. At other times, we have easily dismissed the history of theology as a history of errors and wanderings of other theological traditions. Protestants, thus, have had the tendency to look at our past as mostly compromised and tainted by Roman Catholic "heresies." If history is mostly a succession of theological errors, its study may not be very necessary or important. There is also great complexity in the historical endeavour. We interact with ancient sources and languages, we attempt to understand the development of ideas and concepts, all the while thinking and "doing" theology in our own context.

Through this process, we constantly look back at the ages which precede us, and we cast a positive or a critical eye on them. We label them, categorise them and learn from them. In the history of Europe certain periods are given names to help students and teachers alike identify an epoch. We can speak of "Antiquity" or "Late Antiquity", the "Renaissance" or the "Reformation". Some will have identifiable beginnings or endings. Others will lack that precision but gradually blend from one age into another. One stands out in the list of epochs not only because of its length but because of its name: "The Dark Ages". It is more than a description. It is a condemnation.

Although without absolute certainty, the person to whom that particular expression is attributed is Petrarch. Francesco Petrarca lived in the fourteenth century and was a scholar and poet of the early Italian Renaissance. His rediscovery of the letters of Cicero may have been something of the catalyst for the Renaissance in the same way that the 95 Theses nailed to the door of All Saints Church in Wittenberg gives a start date for the Reformation. For some scholars the term applies to A.D. 500-1000. In a broader sense the Dark Ages are sometimes taken to stretch from Late Antiquity to the Renaissance, that is from A.D. 500-1300.

In calling this extended period of time "Dark" the historian or philosopher is actually making a judgement not only about the epoch but about what came before and after. A Renaissance writer might look back wistfully towards the days of Ancient Rome with a degree of reverence lamenting its demise. Rome stood as a symbol of civilisation eclipsed by the rampaging hordes who rushed in at its collapse to extinguish its light. When Rome fell, darkness engulfed the continent, relieved only by the return to classical studies that marked the Renaissance.

We should not, however, be too quick to simply use the nomenclature that passes judgement on this period without examining some of the evidence. Though "the glory that was Rome" can certainly be inspiring and the examples of its architecture engage both head and heart even to this day, not all that was done in its name was laudable. It has been estimated that 20–30 per cent of the population of Roman society were enslaved. Entertainment included spectating as one man tried, and often succeeded, to kill another. Unwanted children were simply abandoned. The sick were thought to be under the curse of the gods and were left to either recover or simply die.

The fêted eighteenth-century scholar and classicist, Edward Gibbon, may have blamed the Church for the demise of the Roman Empire, but it was Christians who rescued abandoned infants, contrary to the law of the Senate, and raised them as their own. It was the Christian Church that established hospitals to look after the sick and tend to their needs. Up until very recently senior nurses in British hospitals were referred to as "sisters." They fulfilled the same role that nuns in hospitals had performed for a millennium and more.

Perhaps the light of civilisation did not burn as brightly as some of the classicists or some moderns would have us believe. Contrariwise, perhaps the descent into gloom was not as comprehensive or as deep as one might suppose. The Early Middle Ages, or the start of the so-called "Dark Ages", saw a number of significant advances: the heavy plough, the horse collar, and metal horseshoes. Charlemagne (748–814), or Charles the Great, truly deserved the title. It was he who standardised written script, introducing the Carolingian minuscule.

In theology we witness similar lights starting to rise above the horizon. Some of them, like Boethius, Anselm, or Wycliffe, will be the subject of this book. Others, like Thomas Aquinas or Bradwardine will not, though they stand as giants in our theological past. The former do not simply stand as lights in the darkness, but as figures contesting the label itself. When we discover them, we realise that they are the witnesses of an age that was far from dark. Labelling an age "dark" is often a way to cover our own ignorance. Darkness does at times cover the earth, though not in a strictly temporal manner, and not always where we think it does.

*

Our concern in this book is with the Protestant evangelical reading of Church history, or to be more specific, with the appreciation of our theological past. Protestants often have the intuitive tendency to identify the history of the Church by its theological errors. We are prone to see first and foremost the problems, dangers, and unfaithfulness and completely miss out the benefits, the perseverance and the other faithful credal affirmations. We see the heterodoxy and miss the orthodoxy, and we pride ourselves with being on the right side of the medieval age. In doing so, we do not listen to the Christian wisdom of those who preceded us.

It serves no purpose, however, to accumulate guilt upon guilt. Whilst we have often seen the darkness in history instead of seeing the light through the centuries, the said history is not a simple "black" and "white" set of theological affirmations or heretical deviations. Let us leave culpability behind and move towards a better and more balanced appreciation of our heritage. To do so, however, we must also be conscious of the complex developmental nature of theology throughout the ages.

The great Reformed theologian, Francis Turretin, helpfully distinguishes between the "substance of the faith" and the "corrupting accidents in doctrine and worship". Maybe it is time we do so in our own personal theological endeavours, in our church life, and in our theological education as well. We should also train ourselves to look for the "unexpected" truth, contrary to what we might initially think. We should train our theological minds to see the best first, instead of the worst. We should live out the principle of charity: assume the faithful and orthodox interpretation, be aware that no theology is perfect, be appreciative of the Church's struggle for orthodoxy.

This is our goal in this book: we want to show that there has always been a thread running through history, including through the medieval age. This thread is the constant struggle for an orthodox, faithful, and glorifying theology: one that gives God due honour, that takes Scripture as the principal authority over life and faith, and that nourishes our wonder and worship. The Middle Ages also were brightened by the light of the Gospel, the same light that shines every time we remain faithful to Scripture's "good deposit".

This is easier said than done, however. Or rather, it can be done the simple way, or the better way. After all, it is easy (or relatively so) to go back in time, pick up a few good things here and there: one of Bernard of Clairvaux's sermons on the love of God, one of Augustine's treatises on the primacy of grace, or a quote from Thomas Aquinas on the nature of faith. It is more difficult to strive to *recover* the history of our Christian theology. To do so, we must not pick and choose a few "affirmative" moments of the Church but see how theology has developed through an historical process. We should learn to listen to what the theologians are concerned about, which challenges they try to answer, and with whom they interact.

Our goal is thus not to suggest that the theologians we will present were perfect, nor that they had a pure theology. Of course not. Incidentally, neither is ours. No theology is without stain, approximations, and can even lead to relative misunderstandings. That is inherent to the theological task. Nor is our goal to paint these theologians as pre-reformers, as if the Reformations of the sixteenth century were the only lens through which to read Church history. We must learn to read the theologians of the Medieval Church for themselves. We must read them for who they were and what they wrote—without labelling them as orthodox or heretics.

Our desire is to delve into our common Church history and be thankful witnesses of the continuing presence of true theology and faithfulness to the God of the Scriptures. In arguing so, we do not want to overstate the differences between, for example, Thomas Aquinas and his contemporaries. Our goal is not to paint one theologian as the only repository of orthodoxy, over against all the other theologians of his age. The ten figures we offer here should not be seen as the only orthodox teachers of the Medieval Church, but as representatives of the continuity of faithful pilgrim theology (*theologia viatorum*). We present them as examples of a broader aim: discerning the continuing thread of faithful theology, done in an attitude of humble hearing, reading, and meditation on the Scriptures.

*

Our modest attempt at reclaiming this millennium follows ten main figures of the Medieval Church. To do so, we will pay special attention to the world in which our theologians lived and wrote, as well as some biographical background. This book is not just about facts of the past however. It is also about the history of Christian theology. What we try to do is to encourage every one of us to look at the past as a living witness to God's providence. We can learn from the theologians of the past for there has always been faithful teaching. We propose to point to several aspects of medieval theology which remain as relevant and important for us today.

We submit these chapters as theologians interested in Church history. Yannick is first an apologist, earning his doctorate in Apologetics and teaching in that subject. Iain has served as a pastor for over forty years, and has found time to study for a doctorate in historical theology. We are students of the Scriptures, and of history. While not being professional church historians, we both love Church history deeply, because we love Christ's Church. We are drawn to the exercise of humility and reflection that is required by looking deeply into our past, for the past is a great part of who we are. Protestantism as we know it, and even that of the first decade of the Reformation, did not arise without antecedents at the beginning of the sixteenh century. It is one of the descendants of the Medieval Church, just as the Council of Trent subsequently codified Roman Catholic theology.

As Protestant believers we must wrestle with a humble reading of the past, taking the risk of being encouraged, edified, and even corrected, by these medieval theologians. Like these ten figures under review, we are still engaged in the process of reading, writing, and understanding theology after the Ecumenical Councils. Theological faithfulness is not merely something to be preserved after the Reformation, but to be wrestled with, and refined, until all is perfected in the coming of the kingdom. All theology is provisional, including Reformed theology, as was medieval theology. This conviction should accompany our current theological reflections. It is our hope that this contribution will be helpful in that task.

Leo the Great (400-461)

The struggle for Christ's divinity

At the time of the Reformation the two great antagonists were undoubtedly Martin Luther and the pope in Rome. It is hardly surprising, then, that Protestants have often regarded even the mention of a pope with much suspicion. Those suspicions are only fuelled by the historical record of what has come to be known as "The Pornocracy" of the tenth-century popes and the scurrilous record of John XXIII who was eventually deposed and officially classified as an antipope. His deposition by the Council of Constance did not hinder pope Martin V from appointing him a Cardinal, in which office he died. Of John XXIII, Edward Gibbon wrote in his magisterial work on the *Decline and Fall of the Roman Empire*, "The more scandalous charges were suppressed; the vicar of Christ was accused only of piracy, rape, sodomy, murder and incest." No doubt Gibbon, the Enlightenment scholar, was writing with more than a hint of irony, but the point is made: those who had ascended to the throne of St. Peter cannot be regarded universally as men of eminent holiness.

The consequence of a predisposition to view popes with suspicion inevitably asks for a degree of special pleading to place any name on our selective list of those who deserve not only our attention, but also our thanks for holding aloft a torch that still burns brightly after so many centuries. There were undoubtedly many rogues who held the highest ecclesiastical office, and yet there were also those who, in the opinion of the authors of this slim volume were, to coin a phrase, on the side

1

of the angels. One such person was Leo I, also known for good reason as Leo the Great.

Biographical sketch

The origins of Leo more than sixteen centuries ago, are difficult to trace and such details as we might have, are open to question. Some have asserted that he was a lawyer from Tuscany in the north of Italy. Others have claimed just as firmly that he was a Roman. If he was not, in fact, actually from Rome, then he had certainly imbibed its spirit in terms of his proud dignity and bearing. He distinguished himself under popes Celestine I and Sixtus III and obviously enjoyed not only their favour, but their confidence. Indeed, it was while he was absent in Gaul, serving as an archdeacon and legate, that he was unanimously elected pope.

There are two matters for which Leo stands out, and which have rightly earned him the title "the Great". The only other pope to be accorded such a title was Gregory I. The first matter was theological, in that he gave to the Church what has become known as *Leo's Tome,* which became a foundational document for the Second Council of Ephesus in 449, and was even more significant for the Council of Chalcedon (451). What makes the life of Leo even more remarkable was that just three years later, the theologian went out to meet the notorious Attila the Hun face-to-face. The Emperor had removed himself to Constantinople as the new political centre of the Roman world, leaving the pope, by default, to become something of a leading citizen if not *the* leading citizen. United in one person were both a capacity for substantial scholarship and a strength of character that would not shy away from meeting with the most formidable warrior of his age, as he stood poised to destroy Rome itself.

Socio-political and theological context

We will come to the theological significance of Leo shortly but first we should set his pontifical reign in its historical context. Constantine had moved his capital away from Rome to Constantinople (modern-day Istanbul) in 330. No longer the political centre of the "known" world, it fell to the pope to effectively become Rome's leading citizen. Leo ascended the papal throne in 440 at the age of forty. Twelve years later Rome faced the greatest crisis of that generation: Attila the Hun descended on Italy threatening to sack the ancient imperial capital. Attila the Hun is one of the few names of the leaders of the Barbarian hordes to have gone down in history. He was noted for his ferocity and the threat of his approach was more than sufficient to galvanise local leaders into action. It was thus that Leo set out to meet Attila in an effort to dissuade him from destroying Rome. They met on the southern shores of Lake Garda in northern Italy. Shortly after their meeting Attila retreated and the city was saved. There are multiple explanations for this. It is more than possible that Leo carried with him a substantial amount of gold with which he bribed Attila to proceed no further. Other explanations include insufficient food for Attila's soldiers, disease amongst the ranks, and a growing army arriving on the eastern coast of Italy from the Emperor in the East. Most likely each of these played a part in persuading Attila to retreat from Italy. Whatever the cause, it was Leo who was given credit for persuading the invader to turn around and head north. In doing so he greatly enhanced not only his own reputation but the prestige of the papacy.

Though the rise of the papacy is far outside the remit of this work, it has to be admitted that Leo the Great was not unwilling to assert the primacy of the See of Rome over the other centres of Christianity: Constantinople, Jerusalem, Antioch and Alexandria. Later Jerusalem, Antioch and Alexandria would fall to Islam, and Constantinople owed its significance solely to its political importance and had no historical links to the Apostles or to the churches they founded. Those concerns were in the future. In Leo's day, Rome claimed primacy on the grounds of its connections with Paul and especially Peter, whom it viewed as the first pope. This was not coincidental to how Leo dealt with theological divisions. Though we may not be supportive of his claim to be the senior, even sole, custodian of Christian theology, we can at least be thankful that his contribution was on the side of Biblical truth.

Leo's theological contribution

We can now turn to the theological point at issue and examine Leo's contribution and commitment to Biblical orthodoxy particularly as affirmed in the Council of Chalcedon (451). Chalcedon did much to clarify our understanding and define our Christology. At the heart of the debate was the relationship of the human to the divine. Arius (256-336) denied outright the divinity of Christ and therefore the Trinity. His theological successors are with us to this day as Jehovah's Witnesses. If the divinity of Christ is to be maintained, how are we to understand the relationship of the second person of the Trinity to the humanity of Christ? Over the years the church was tugged first in one direction and then in another: at one time emphasising the divinity of Christ at the expense of His humanity, and then as the pendulum would swing in the other direction, emphasising the humanity of Christ at the expense of His divinity. The inclination to go in one direction or the other is understandable. A Jesus who is simply another man, albeit on a significantly elevated level, poses no real intellectual challenge. A Jesus who is simply divine, though this too was to be challenged in the age of the Enlightenment, is relatively easy to digest. When we have a Christology that asserts that Jesus is the unique "*theanthropos*," God-man, then work needs to be done to understand the nature of the union of those two natures—human and divine—in the one person.

Arius' solution did at least have the merit of simplicity. He denied that Jesus possessed absolute divinity. He was opposed by Apollinaris (A.D. 382) who was Bishop of Laodicea. In his desire to maintain the divinity of Christ, he denied the fullness

4

of His humanity. In Apollinaris' view, the divine Logos took the place of the human spirit; the human spirit was the source of sin so by replacing the human spirit with the divine Logos, he sought not only to defend the divinity of Christ but to maintain His sinlessness. The fatal weakness of this line of argument is that the humanity that Apollonaris is proposing is a humanity without a rational dimension. A Jesus without a human rational element is not human as we know it. The implication for our doctrine of salvation, our soteriology, is catastrophic. In an effort to safeguard the divinity of Christ Apollonaris left us with a Saviour who is unable to renew humanity in the totality of its being. He was affirming the divinity of Christ to the detriment of His humanity. Thus, the Alexandrian school came to assert Mary as the *"theotokos"*—as God-bearer. Additionally, it is difficult to escape the Docetic element in Apollonaris' formulation. The origin of the word "Docetism" lies in the Greek word, *dokeo*, meaning "to seem." According to this error, Jesus only "seemed" to be a man but in fact was not fully man as we are. It was in response to this that the Synod of Alexandria (362) used the word "soul" in respect of Christ to include the rational element.

Opposing the Alexandrian view was Theodore of Antioch, often referred to as Theodore of Mopsuestia, who represented Antioch. He denied the essential indwelling of the divine to the extent that the connection of the divine in the person of Christ was not substantively different to the indwelling of the Holy Spirit in the believer. It can be seen by this that while Apollonaris played down the humanity, Theodore was playing down the divinity. Antiochan theology was developed further by Nestorius (386-450) who denied that Mary was the *"theotokos"*. He had concluded she bore only the humanity of Christ. Though it seemingly solved one problem, it raised another: how can Mary have brought forth God? It created an even greater problem as it separated the humanity from the Godhead giving rise to a doctrine of God having assumed the body of Jesus rather than being fully united. Nestorius did not explicitly state this as his position, but his followers were less reluctant to embrace the conclusion.

The Alexandrian School was then represented by Cyril (376–444). Cyril claimed that the logical conclusion of Nestorius' position is that if Mary is not *"theotokos"* then the person to whom she gave birth is not divine. If He is not divine, then God has not become incarnate and in its place we have to talk of the divine assumption of humanity. That changes the nature of Christ's relationship to humanity.

It was not just the singularity of the person of Christ that had to be maintained, it was also the nature of the relationship of the two natures. It was in this latter aspect that Nestorianism failed. While it recognised the two natures—an advance on the Arian heresy—it failed to deal with the nature of the union of the two natures adequately. The separation of the two natures was such that the man, Christ, became no more than a God-bearer and is worthy of worship not because He is God but because God is in Him. Cyril's contribution to Christology was his emphasis on the unity of the Person of Christ. For him the two natures were in indissoluble union while remaining distinct.

A contemporary of Cyril, Eutyches (380–456) sought to define further the doctrine of the two natures by a formula of which Cyril would not have approved. While holding to Christ having two natures, in his opinion the human nature of Christ had been absorbed into the divine. By this fusion a new nature had been created rendering the humanity of Christ no longer consubstantial with our own. In that sense Jesus was not truly human in the proper use of the word. The result was that Eutyches was deposed and excommunicated by the so-called "Robber Council" of Ephesus in 448. As a result, Eutyches appealed to the Bishop of Rome and it was in response to this that Leo wrote what is now referred to as his *Tome*.

Relevance and significance

From the brief history recounted above it can be seen that the swinging of the theological pendulum needed a clear Christological statement to arrest its momentum. That statement came at the Council of Chalcedon (451). It was built, however, on the foundation that Leo laid in his rightly celebrated *Tome* to which we now turn.

Leo begins by giving a clear affirmation of the divinity of Christ:

> ... the whole body of the faithful confess that they believe in GOD the Father Almighty, and in Jesus Christ, His only Son, our LORD, who was born of the Holy Spirit and the Virgin Mary. By which three statements the devices of almost all heretics are overthrown. For not only is GOD believed to be both Almighty and the Father, but the Son is shown to be co-eternal with Him, differing in nothing from the Father because He is GOD from GOD, Almighty from Almighty, and *being born from the Eternal one is co-eternal with Him*; not later in point of time, not lower in power, not unlike in glory, not divided in essence: but at the same time the only begotten of the eternal Father was born eternal of the Holy Spirit and the Virgin Mary. [Emphasis added.]

He goes on to expound upon the two natures of Christ:

> And this nativity which took place in time *took nothing from, and added nothing to that divine and eternal birth*, but expended itself wholly on the restoration of man who had been deceived: in order that he might both vanquish death and overthrow by his strength, the Devil who possessed the power of death. For we should not now be able to overcome the author of sin and death unless He took our nature on Him and made it His own, whom neither sin could pollute nor death retain. Doubtless then, He was conceived of the Holy Spirit within the womb of His Virgin Mother, who brought Him forth without the loss

of her virginity, even as she conceived Him without its loss. [Emphasis added.]

And that those two natures are united in one person:

> [Eutyches held] that the Word became flesh in such a way that Christ, born of the Virgin's womb, had the form of man, but had not the reality of His mother's body. Or is it possible that he thought our LORD Jesus Christ was not of our nature for this reason, that the angel, who was sent to the blessed Mary ever Virgin, says, "The Holy Ghost shall come upon thee and the power of the Most High shall overshadow thee: and therefore that Holy Thing also that shall be born of thee shall be called the Son of GOD," on the supposition that as the conception of the Virgin was a Divine act, the flesh of the conceived did not partake of the conceiver's nature? But that birth so uniquely wondrous and so wondrously unique, is not to be understood in such wise that the properties of His kind were removed through the novelty of His creation. For though the Holy Spirit imparted fertility to the Virgin, yet a real body was received from her body; and, "Wisdom building her a house," "the Word became flesh and dwelt in us,' that is, *in that flesh which he took from man and which he quickened with the breath of a higher life.*" [Emphasis added.]

In a most memorable phrase Leo declares that the "emptying of Himself whereby the Invisible made Himself visible and, creator and LORD of all things though He be, wished to be a mortal, was the bending down of pity, not the failing of power."

Leo is succinctly building a clear Christology that Jesus is fully God and that He is fully man. In His person two natures are united and from that flows the *communicatio idiomatum* which holds that what can be said of either His human or His divine attributes may correctly be referred to the other nature.

> Without detriment therefore to the *properties of either nature and substance which then came together in one person, majesty took on humility, strength weakness, eternity mortality: and for the paying off*

of the debt belonging to our condition inviolable nature was united with passible nature, so that, as suited the needs of our case, one and the same Mediator between GOD and men, the Man Christ Jesus, could both die with the one and not die with the other. Thus in the whole and perfect nature of true man was true GOD born, complete in what was His own, complete in what was ours. [Emphasis added.]

As Leo continues his Christology he affirms that redemption required that the mediator be both fully God and fully man, anticipating the argument of Anselm in *Cur Deus Homo?* by almost 600 years.

And not undeservedly was he pronounced blessed by the LORD, drawing from the chief corner-stone the solidity of power which his name also expresses, he, who, through the revelation of the Father, confessed Him to be at once Christ and Son of GOD: *because the receiving of the one of these without the other was of no avail to salvation*, and it was equally perilous to have believed the LORD Jesus Christ to be either only GOD without man, or only man without GOD. [Emphasis added.]

Leo concludes that the union of man with God is indissoluble; that the second person of the Trinity did not assume human form temporarily but continues fully man as well as fully God:

So again He showed the wound in His side, the marks of the nails, and all the signs of His quite recent suffering, saying, "See My hands and feet, that it is I. Handle Me and see that a spirit hath not flesh and bones, as ye see Me have;" in order that the properties of His Divine and human nature might be acknowledged *to remain still inseparable*: and that we might know the Word not to be different from the flesh, in such a sense as also to confess that the one Son of GOD is both the Word and flesh. [Emphasis added.]

What is also particularly striking about the way in which Leo writes is his constant use of Scripture. In the *Tome* which runs to a little over 3,000 words there are in the region of three dozen citations of Scripture. Leo is not appealing to his own authority as the Bishop of Rome or to the Church Fathers but seeking to argue from what the Scriptures teach.

Now, compare the Confession of Chalcedon (451) with what Leo set down:

> We, then, following the holy Fathers, all with one consent, teach people to confess one and the same Son, our Lord Jesus Christ, the same perfect in Godhead and also perfect in manhood; truly God and truly man, of a reasonable [rational] soul and body; consubstantial [co-essential] with the Father according to the Godhead, and consubstantial with us according to the Manhood; in all things like unto us, without sin; begotten before all ages of the Father according to the Godhead, and in these latter days, for us and for our salvation, born of the Virgin Mary, the Mother of God, according to the Manhood; one and the same Christ, Son, Lord, only begotten, to be acknowledged in two natures, inconfusedly, unchangeably, indivisibly, inseparably; the distinction of natures being by no means taken away by the union, but rather the property of each nature being preserved, and concurring in one Person and one Subsistence [the hypostatic union], not parted or divided into two persons, but one and the same Son, and only begotten God, the Word, the Lord Jesus Christ; as the prophets from the beginning [have declared] concerning Him, and the Lord Jesus Christ Himself has taught us, and the Creed of the holy Fathers has handed down to us.

From this we see that the Confession of Chalcedon leaned heavily upon the theology set out by Leo.

Conclusion

There are undoubtedly matters with which a good many would wish to take issue. Leo's insistence on the primacy of the See of Rome over the other Patriarchates would prove to be a considerable stumbling block especially when subsequent occupants of the same office proved so reprehensible. We should, however, note that his insistence is also set in particular political circumstances. With the removal of the Emperor to the capital in the East, the pope in Rome *de facto* became something akin to "First Citizen". It was in that role that pope Leo found himself face-to-face with one of the bloodiest leaders of his, or indeed, of any other generation. That historians have suggested contributing factors to Attila's decision to withdraw does not detract from the fact that, whatever the conditions, Leo was by no means assured of the outcome. He did not flee from Rome and hide himself away. He went and met Attila even at the risk of his own life. That must surely command our respect. But there is more. He had a clear grasp of biblical theology, argued from Scripture and for that he deserves our thanks.

·

Boethius (476–524)

Trusting God's providence

Biographical sketch

Boethius was born to an aristocratic family during troubled times. Around the time of his birth, in 476, the Visigoth chief Odovacar deposed the last Roman emperor, marking the end of a centuries-long era of Roman cultural and political dominance. After the transfer of the imperial capital to Constantinople (324–330), Rome rapidly lost its position as the heart of the empire. This was the result of the Gothic incursions and the initial sack of Rome which occurred in 410. These incursions led to the fragmentation of the Roman Empire at the hands of Gothic tribes, leading to ever-changing political alliances. Even while the emperor at Constantinople remained the supreme ruler, at least nominally, local chiefs and governors became *de facto* the real civil power. By the time of Boethius' birth, Rome had ceased to be the glorious city of the Caesars of our imagination.

Around 488, the young Boethius became orphaned, and was then raised by senator Symmachus, even becoming his son-in-law. His guardian was himself one of the most important Senators of the time, and a pivotal figure of the Roman aristocracy. A few years after becoming Symmachus' ward, a political event occurred that would shape Boethius' public life. In 493, the Ostrogoth king Theodoric (454–526) murdered Odoacer, emperor Zeno's viceroy in Italy, and replaced him. Rapidly, the young scholar became part of Theodoric's government, even though the specifics as to his nomination remain unclear.

Given Boethius' rare expertise in Hellenic culture and the Greek language, it is highly possible that he came to the attention of Theodoric when he visited Rome in 500. From what we can gather from Theodoric's correspondence, it is not only Boethius' Hellenic and linguistic achievements which brought him to the king's attention, but also his reputation as a man of education and culture.

Around 510, Boethius became the consul of Rome, and was introduced to the senate and honoured as a patrician; a rare title for someone so young. The fact that he was so close to the Roman senate and had won their recognition certainly created some suspicions within Theodoric's circle as to where Boethius' political loyalties lay. His fame continued to rise, as did that of his family, and his two sons were appointed joint consuls in 522; a great distinction and recognition of the three men's service. During that time, Boethius would devote an important part of his days to his lifelong project of translating and commenting on Greek philosophical texts (mostly Aristotle) for a Latin audience.

In 522-523, he was appointed "Master of Offices", a prestigious and demanding position whose responsibilities included chief of the palace guard, head of the civil service, director of the postal service, and he also served as the equivalent of the Secretary of State. In short, Boethius became the single most important official figure in Theodoric's government, acting as the representative of the Ostrogoth king. This key position gave him the opportunity to live according to his faith and ethical standards, defending the oppressed and strongly opposing corruption at court, which Boethius himself sees, in *The Consolation of Philosophy*, as one of the reasons for his downfall.

Not long after being named Master of Offices, Boethius was accused of conspiring against Theodoric. This sudden fall from such a high position started with the accusations brought against senator Albinus, who had been charged with entertaining treasonable correspondence with Constantinople officials close to Emperor Justin. As Master of Offices, it was likely Boethius' responsibility to bring Albinus to trial, but instead of acting as prosecutor, he defended the Roman official, raising questions of possible collusion with the accused.

In the *Consolation*, he gives us a precise explanation as to the three accusations made against him. Firstly, he was accused of suppressing the evidence against Albinus: ironically, a charge of corruption. Secondly, Boethius was accused of writing letters defending, and longing for, Roman liberty: a charge of treason. Finally, he was accused of practicing magic: a religious charge. Despite his defence, Boethius was tried, convicted and imprisoned by the very same Senate he was accused of treasonably supporting. After some time, he was executed along with Symmachus, his father-in-law.

Socio-political and theological context

To understand Boethius's work better, as well as the tragic end of his life, we must also consider these early times in which he lived. Four key elements of Theodoric's reign are particularly important to remember.

The first key dimension of Theodoric's reign is that he displayed true leadership, at least for a time. His pragmatic rule allowed him to reason, and make alliances with parties that were initially not natural allies. For example, he married the sister of Clovis, who had himself married a princess from a tribe that confessed the orthodox Chalcedonian creed, and not a form of Arianism like so many other tribes. Theodoric's daughters were given in marriage to other tribal chiefs, thus securing political alliances that allowed him to establish himself as the most important ruler in the West. In fact, by Theodoric's death in 526, all the lands that had formerly been part of the Western Roman Empire (with the exception of parts of Gaul and of Britain) were under the authority of a single ruler.

Theodoric's leadership meant, secondly, that he was far from being a stereotypical Barbarian. Like many rulers of the late Fifth and early Sixth centuries, he had a fascination for the collapsing Roman culture, to the point that he strove to keep the Roman consulate alive, even if mostly in a ceremonial fashion. This led the Roman aristocracy to align more closely with Theodoric's interest: it was theirs also. Under Theodoric's leadership there was greater peace, order, and security, and with that a greater level of prosperity. His love of Roman culture led to a revival of learning.

While being counted as one of the invading tribal leaders of the Goths, Theodoric was a Christian, albeit an Arian Christian, but perceived as a member of the new faith nonetheless. This religious dimension of Theodoric's reign is the third main aspect of his rule. He had embraced the "Roman religion" which, by the end of the fifth century, was Christianity. Even though he was Arian, he had enough political sense to realise that uniting Romans and Goths under his rule demanded that he place orthodox Christians in key positions in his government, one of whom was Boethius.

Finally, the reign of Theodoric was plagued by tense relations with the emperor, a political situation which was aggravated by continuing theological debates over Christology. While the unity of the human and the divine natures of the person of Christ, the mediator, was officially resolved at the Council of Chalcedon (451), the Council failed to bring about immediate theological unity. Because of the intricate relationship between society, state, and religion, the promotion of the Chalcedonian faith rested partly on the power of the empire. Unfortunately, the Byzantine Empire was, at the time, unable to exert enough control to enforce the newly attained theological formulation in its Eastern provinces. The Emperor could not, however, remain passive when faced with the social tension threatening the integrity of the empire itself. Theodoric, for his part, was tempted to use the influence of Arian tribes to push his bid for power. When Emperor Justin started persecuting Arians in the East who denied the divinity of Christ, Theodoric in retaliation took measures against "Catholics."

When we consider this context, Boethius's involvement in the Christological debate of the early sixth century should also be seen as charged with political implications. Someone in his official position could never be seen as only a theologian when he wrote theological treatises, and a statesman when he worked on government affairs. Such a separation was not only foreign to the times, but also impossible to maintain in practice. Boethius's enemies benefited from Theodoric's change of fortune. His position had weakened since the Eastern emperor had resolved the differences that threatened to divide Eastern and Western Christians. At the same time, the Emperor promoted a rigid opposition to Arian Christians—one of whom was Theodoric. During the same time, a pro-Byzantine pope was elected, further weakening Theodoric's position. It is easy to understand why every attempt to bridge the differences between West and East could be interpreted as pro-Byzantine activity, and could be considered by Theodoric as treason. That explains in part the fall of Boethius: his defence of theological orthodoxy, which was not politically motivated, could be, and was, used by his political opponents.

Works and legacy

Boethius's relevance for us can only be explained when we see him as standing firmly within the Christian faith, while at the same time relying on, benefiting from, and deeply appreciating the pagan philosophers who came before him. Neoplatonism was one of the most influential philosophical traditions, formative of Boethius's intellectual and spiritual life. The Neoplatonic philosopher Proclus had died in 485, when Boethius was a teenager. According to him, all things are directed towards the One ultimate source of goodness, which is itself the desire of all human beings. Typical also of Neoplatonism is the metaphor of voyage or ascent, when the Soul discovers its real origin and destination. This would inform Boethius's *Consolation of Philosophy*. Neoplatonist philosopher Porphyry was also significant for Boethius because he had been largely responsible for making Aristotelian logic a central subject in the Neoplatonic curriculum. This logic would be central to Boethius's scholarly endeavour.

Boethius's philosophical and theological works could puzzle his readers. The two sides of his writings can seem totally isolated from each other. Many scholars have noted that there seems to be a certain tension in Boethius's lifelong intellectual endeavours. The most telling example of such tension is the absence of conscious and direct reference to his Christian faith in the *Consolation of Philosophy*. How are we to explain this tension? Was Boethius less Christian than we actually think? As he was imprisoned, was his only hope in death to be found in philosophical consolation—and not in his faith?

One answer is to simply take those texts at face value. That is what C. S. Lewis did, writing that Boethius did *not* look for the consolation of his religion, but of philosophy, and that he wrote not religiously, but philosophically. Was Boethius merely concerned with affairs of reason and not faith?

The perspective of Lewis, at least superficially, seems convincing. This, of course, could isolate reason from faith. Moreover, it underestimates the philosophical nature of some of his theological treatises, including Boethius's attempt to bring Aristotelian categories to bear on the defence of orthodox trinitarian thought. Through their instrumentality, Boethius attempted to demonstrate the Trinity's unity and self-sufficiency, showing that reason and faith were connected. The simple separation between two fields of writing—one theological, the other philosophical—also underestimates the limited value of philosophy in *The Consolation* with respect to eternal blessedness.

Another reason for the distinction between philosophical and theological works is to observe that they belong to two different orders and domains of understanding: natural and doctrinal investigations, done respectively through reason and faith. There is certainly ground in Boethius for such a division.

But it is not the whole story. Another part of the answer lies both in Boethius's Christian faith, and in the Neoplatonic intuition about the structure of the world. The former confessed that the world had a created structure that it owed to a providential and benevolent God, who was the *summum bonum* of human life. The latter stressed not a Christian view of the world, but philosophical conclusions that were congruent with the Christian faith.

Neoplatonism presented a cosmic worldview, regulated by order, harmony, and virtues, directed towards perfect goodness. It also provided a structure of argumentation and logical categories through which Boethius thought he could strengthen the case for the Christian faith. A case in point was logic itself. Logic is not the result of Neoplatonic thought. What Neoplatonism discovered and formulated was not a new or a humanly created order, but the very same order that the God of his Christian faith created.

The tension often seen in Boethius' dual domains of writing, (i.e. philosophy and theology), was not so evident to him. This is not to say that he did not see any tensions between his philosophical interests and his Christian faith. Several times in the *Consolation*, Boethius the narrator shows himself quite conscious of the limitations of philosophy. Its comforts and consolations might only be pedagogical, leading towards, and pointing to the ultimate and most perfect consolation of all.

In writing in such a way, Boethius was doing nothing different from what earlier generations of theologians had been doing: bringing philosophy and theology together. He follows in the footsteps of Church Father Clement of Alexandria and apologist Mincius Felix who both, albeit differently, attempted to establish a connection between Greek philosophy and Christian thought. There is no absolute opposition between the two, because *truth*, which can be arrived at rationally, can never be opposed to *revealed truth*. For Boethius though, philosophical articulation never suffices to establish the truth of doctrine. In fact, closing his treatise on the Trinity, *The Trinity is One God Not Three Gods*, he warns that he only *intended* to present the truth of the faith.

Theology was not merely one aspect of his intellectual endeavours, but its highest form. Philosophy could serve theology. The principles of reason can confirm (not as *validating* but as *affirming*), or point to, doctrinal affirmations. Reason and faith are not two instruments independently leading to truth, but do so conjointly. This has always been a widespread attitude of the Christian tradition: philosophy has never been rejected as having no value at all. Christian theologians have explained the value of philosophy in very different ways. What is essential to see here is that philosophy and theology are never completely isolated from each other.

Focus and relevance

The relevance of Boethius owes much to the influence of his major work, *The Consolation of Philosophy*, and especially to the spiritual path taken by Boethius under the guidance of Lady Philosophy. Written while he was imprisoned because of false charges, this work is structured along a specific pattern of Greek literature, alternating prose and poetry. Scholars continue to debate how to read the *Consolation*, though with such a complex work, there will inevitably be a variety of ways to approach it. One of them is to read it as it first appears to us: a philosophical voyage leading from worldly ruin to the ascending discovery of truth and goodness.

Another way is to take into account the ironic nature of the literary genre adopted by Boethius. In such a view, the narrator's role is not merely to be the student of Lady Philosophy, but to be the tool through whom the author will unveil the limitations of philosophy itself. This leads Boethius, the author, to recognise earthly goods as what they are, things that do not provide lasting happiness. Under the guidance of Lady Philosophy, Boethius the narrator will be led on a spiritual ascent towards the vision of the good, loving, and providential God.

This journey is not unique to him. The disconnection between what we see in the world—pain, suffering, injustice, and death—and what we believe—in a God who cares for his creation, and in particular for his people—can at times unsettle us. When we see Boethius lamenting over his loss of power and status, we naturally relate to his human despair. As he is blinded by sorrow and grief, so we can be when we are faced with great tragedy of which we cannot make sense. At other times, we suffer because of injustice—real or perceived. That was also the case for Boethius, imprisoned for doing what was right and just. This sense of injustice can come in varied forms, including not getting what we think we are owed.

The first lesson Boethius learned from Lady Philosophy is that much of the pain and evil affecting his life, came from not being in accord with his nature (Book I). We desire things, but we use the wrong name to talk about them. We desire wealth, power, and fame, but that which we desire is actually not *true* wealth, power, and fame. The problem is that he is using the wrong words for what his soul really desires. What Boethius must reacquire is knowledge of the cosmos' ultimate cause—his ultimate cause—that towards which we incline and by which alone the ultimate goal, and happiness, can be found. As such Boethius's only consolation, as also found throughout the history of Christian theology, is to throw himself into the arms of God, the efficient cause of creation. This God is the one who will give true meaning to what we are longing for.

Our path towards complete faith in the caring God, master of the universe, is to name Him as providential Lord. What Boethius discovered is that seeing God as the cause of all that exists in the world leads to one great implication: the God of providence has to be confessed not as an abstract ruler of the world, but the personal ruler of our own lives (Book II). He does not only providentially rule the history of salvation, ruling over the major events of redemption, but also over everything that happens in the world. He is always providential, never sleeping, always guiding.

Such radical embrace of God's loving providence is not easy to attain. Obstacles stand in our way. They bear the same names as before: injustice, evil, suffering, disappointments, and doubts. To transform Boethius's vision of the world, Lady Philosophy contrasts the treacherous Wheel of Fortune with God, the unmoved Mover of the Christian faith. He alone, whose nature never changes, should be the model for the believer. He is the "Rock of Ages", against which the changing tides of human affairs will break. The *Consolation* is not an atheological philosophical reflection, but a dialogue between reason and faith, building on philosophy's limitations in order to direct the narrator to the path of consolation. Personal divine providence is what Boethius should keep his eyes fixed upon, not illusory and treacherous human Fortune.

It is also what we should keep our eyes focused upon. The God who created the world, who gives life, who guides and redeems—the God who comes in Christ and sends His Spirit—is the one who is never surprised by what happens. He is the mysterious, unseen hand active in the world in ways that are often incomprehensible to man.

Does that mean that the things of the world are nothing? Do wealth, power, and fame, hold nothing but illusory promises? Providence, as explained by Lady Philosophy, leads us to humility and worship, because it is not always, maybe not often, rationally or immediately apprehended. We should live God's providence by proper use and enjoyment of good things. We should also strive to see the value in *bad* fortunes, rather than only expect lasting happiness from the *good* ones. Earthly goods are only that; earthly ornaments that cannot lead to lasting happiness. Lady Philosophy does not reject the limited value of temporal goods, as long as they are seen for what they are. Not to do so is the root of Boethius's discontent, and of our own.

Trusting in God's providence is a great article of faith that infuses our daily life with a sense of God's mysterious presence. How can we learn this truth? We must remember that all earthly values—justice, love, wealth, fame—and even their absence, can be understood when they lead and point towards God, the *summum bonum*. He is the highest good and ultimate centre of gravity of man's desperate quest (Book III). Lady Philosophy, working as a spiritual counsellor, is directing our spiritual gaze towards God who, as creator, is the one in whom all find true form and meaning.

In the most famous poem of the *Consolation*, Boethius makes a confession common to the great Christian tradition: everything that exists has its source in the perfections of God. They seek their proper place. They are turned towards the greatest good, who is centre of it all, the Creator God Himself. He is the only "stable order", who embraces everything and through whom everything is brought into being and has its end. Through this wisdom-tutored philosophical reflection, Boethius is exhorted to be part of this movement through which all return to God in a cosmic participation. God as Lord is our highest and supreme good.

Once again, we do not find here only a theological statement, but the essence of life under God; a conviction that transforms our daily existence. If we confess God's providential care only when He gives us what we want, where is our trust? Or will we confess trust and love in the face of suffering and adversity? How could we be made more and more like Christ, who was the man of suffering and supremely lived in trust and confidence in the providential guidance of His heavenly Father? If we trust in God's providence only when trust is easy, how would we grow to the stature of the Lord who trusted even through suffering and death? The school of providence is where our trust is tested.

At this point, the Christian reader will certainly ask *the* question which comes our way every single time we confess the providential goodness of God. If the Governor of all things is goodness itself, how can there be so much evil in the world, and how can injustice go unpunished? Reflecting on this sensitive question, Boethius makes several observations which will condition his possibility of finding true goodness and happiness. Man must confess the simplicity of Providence, under the good and just direction of an active and constantly present God (Book IV). He is not an abstract Fate, a mechanical causality that can easily be apprehended. Providence is divine reason, an ordering will.

For Boethius's Lady Philosophy, everything depends on His providence, even righteous punishment, which is a demonstration that the wicked are separated from goodness—God. The believer, by contrast, participates in the divine harmony of providence: God is not only the one who governs, but the one who orders the world—even *through* evil. Thus, even adversity and suffering are works of a providentially good God who exercises the believer, strengthens his trust, and sharpens his love. The so-called prosperity that the wicked of the world enjoy—motivated as they are by hate, envy, and gain—is a treacherous one. Boethius discovers in Book IV of the *Consolation* that the promises of Fortune are false. God, through His providence, is never false. We might not understand the workings of God's actions, but that does not mean He is absent. That is why trust in God's providence is not the result of evidential or rational reasoning. It is a matter of faith.

Boethius's journey, our journey, is almost finished, but not quite yet. One could wonder whether, even under the loving care of God, human freedom is still real. How can man be free under the eye of an ever-present providential God? How can prayer be relevant if God is the unmoved Mover and originator of all things? These questions led to one confession: God and man are different beings. Boethius, and the believer along with him, must recognise that humans never see the complete cosmic picture. Many events appear to us as a mere result of chance or bad luck because we have a very limited view of the world.

By contrast, God sees everything at once, and man must become conscious of the great difference between himself and his creator. In most theological questions, rather than concluding that the human mind *cannot understand* God, or that it can *always know* truth, man should acknowledge that in being and in knowledge of the world, God is different. This leads Boethius to confess that God's knowledge is never caused by something outside of Himself, which seems counter-intuitive. In fact if nothing else causes knowledge in God, that would imply that God's decisions are never taken because of something other than Himself. Though this may lead us to suppose that, if God foresees evil He would thus be the sole cause of evil, it is not the case. Here, the guidance of Lady Philosophy breaks down. She cannot help Boethius to grasp how this can be confessed: man is freely responsible for his actions; God is the source of all things, while not being the cause of evil. Ultimately, God is the providential creator and guide, who demands our faith in His ever-watchful care. We meet here again the radical confidence of faith!

Conclusion

In Boethius's most influential work, we meet a confirmed orthodox Christian who did not find it antithetical to his faith to serve in a political world which was far from perfect, or entirely Christian. We discover a believer who lived at a pivotal time of history even though, like every single individual who lives through such times, he could not control the events that unfolded. But he could trust in God's providence.

The *Consolation* is a great confession of God's providence, of man's humility in the face of a world he cannot fully grasp or completely master. Events in the world often seem to us uncontrollable happenings. Only God is fully in control over events and people. Boethius's well-known book is also a recognition of the usefulness of philosophy, but also of its limited nature. In fact, some of the great questions of our Christian lives cannot be satisfactorily answered without the confession of the Christian God. The exercise of our rational abilities can never suffice to reach final conclusions about the relationship between God and His creation. Our reason is limited—not useless, but limited. Boethius's Lady Philosophy was a pedagogue, pointing to our own limitations, and to the humbling confession that God, despite our doubts, uncertainties, and sufferings, will always remain our greatest good; the one in whom we will find everything we truly long for.

This great affirmation meets us in the daily struggles of our Christian life. God is our greatest good, and He leads us back to Him through His providential care. The goods of this life can be His instruments, as can hardships. Our vocation is not to decide what God can use to accomplish His will, but to confess that His will is always at work, even when our minds and hearts do not seem able to accept it.

Alcuin (735–804)

Adoption in Christ

Biographical sketch

Alcuin was born about 735 near York, Northumbria, an area covering the North-East corner of what became England. As a child he attended the cathedral school founded in that city by Archbishop Egbert, an admirer of Bede the Venerable (673–735). Alcuin himself, as a Northumbrian living in the shadow of Bede, could only be influenced by the great monk, whom he considered to be the last of the Church Fathers.

Alcuin's learning was deeply marked by the continuing influence of Bede, from whom he learned the importance of expounding the Bible and studying history. Alcuin became convinced that the eternal and the spiritual were never dissociated from material realities. The historical was not a mere matter of human events: it stood at the intersection of human experience and God's eternal presence. As such, it was where God's providence could be seen at work. A confession of God's ordering of events is an essential part of a healthy spiritual life. This challenges the materialistic view of history. Whether we see it clearly or not, human history is spiritual in nature, because it is God-directed.

During his training, Alcuin showed great abilities, though it was not only his intellectual capacity that brought him to the attention of the archbishop, but also his deep and vibrant piety. Not much is known of that part of the young scholar's life. We know that he was chosen to be director of the school where he had studied. It is actually truly remarkable that he was chosen at only thirty-two. He was then already considered a very pious man, and a great educator, convinced that knowledge was of vital importance to the growth of the individual, and to the flourishing of a culture. Education was not only formal, but also spiritual, and never disconnected from its goal. When he became head of the school, it needed a spiritual as well as an intellectual director. With Alcuin, the school was given both.

Alcuin's life changed in 781, when he met Charlemagne after the king had conquered a great part of Italy. Alcuin's reputation was already spreading, and it did not take Charlemagne much time to invite the Northumbrian scholar to take up residence at the court and become the "Master of the Palace School." Alcuin was not the only great European mind invited by Charlemagne to join the royal court. The king was trying to attract scholars from all over Europe in an attempt to recreate a culture of learning, a sort of new European Athens that could guide the rest of the world on a path of knowledge, culture, and peace.

During the next ten years he was given several missions by Charlemagne, while trying to set up schools throughout the king's dominions. In 786 he returned to his native shores to deal with important ecclesiastical affairs developing there. On the continent, the spread of Christianity continued among Saxon tribes, who had been the last to receive the faith. The Saxons had already been baptised a few years earlier and in certain parts the new faith was taking root. All in all, at the beginning of the 790s Alcuin could be cautiously optimistic about that mission in the West. However, the situation was volatile.

The Saxons were tempted to return to their ancient religion. In his desire to unite Europe, the king could not accept that the Saxons could stay outside the faith. He demanded cooperation of political and spiritual powers in the formation of a new culture. Reacting to Charlemagne's threats the Saxons then reinitiated war with the king. This led to violence on both sides. Saxons killed for the sake of revenge, and Christians in the name of religion and culture. Harsh remarks were made by Christian priests: the Saxons were not to be trusted because they had fallen back into their pagan beliefs. In the next century, Gottschalk, another Saxon, would bear the weight of this mistrust. Alcuin thought a more compassionate approach was needed. Listening to the Saxons, the educator concluded that it was excessive tithing, done in the name of Christianity, that had smothered the young faith of the Saxon tribe. Logically enough, they associated the "new faith" with socio-political powers. The faith was disconnected from the Lord who was supposed to be at its heart. While it would have been easy for Alcuin merely to enjoy his position at the royal court, he prudently questioned the Frankish Emperor when he thought it was necessary. In particular he protested, albeit in a very diplomatic manner, against the royal policy of coercing baptism for the Saxons.

To Alcuin, if Charlemagne wanted to become a European David, he had to exercise justice and mercy, two great virtues consistent with the figure of a "Christian king". In particular, Saxons had to be instructed in the new faith before they could be baptised. The Christian ritual could never be a mere social instrument, or it would be at the expense of its real significance. Baptism without faith, was of no use. Baptism was an act of faith, arising from the free will of the soul. Faith could never be extracted by force, and neither should be the administration of baptism. He concluded that only instruction in faith, love, and self-denial, were the legitimate means for converting the Saxons—or any other pagan tribe.

In what was a controversial social move, Alcuin argued that Saxons should also be instructed in the Christian faith before they were required to pay tithes to their new political lord. Alcuin's criticism of the use of force to impose conversion was not only understandable, but also quite necessary. Alcuin rested his criticism on the most important consideration: the souls of the Saxons were at stake. What should never be lost was the soul, not even if that came at a social or financial loss for the civil power. Charlemagne was dubious at first, though he did not ignore his counsellor's opinion. After 797, the Frankish king became more lenient with Saxon leaders.

In 793, when the monastery of the island of Lindisfarne was sacked by Vikings, Alcuin displayed his Christian and monastic wisdom, noting that the real enemy was not external, but internal. He encouraged learning and confidence in God, even though he was personally shaken by the sack of Lindisfarne. This Viking raid led to social and political turmoil in Northumbria, bringing into question the leadership of the civil and religious authorities. This was one of the occasions during which Alcuin assumed the role of a theologian of history. The problem is that this history, of which he was the recorder, was that of current events. As a participant in those events, could Alcuin really serve as historian? Does not writing history demand a certain critical distance? If it did, Alcuin was not yet convinced of it and became more than a recorder of history. He proposed a theology of history. Alcuin, following Bede and even Augustine, tried to envision through all the crises of Carolingian society a unified world, a history over which God would reign.

The next year, Alcuin attended the Synod of Frankfurt and took an important part in the framing of the decrees condemning Adoptionism, of which we will talk in more detail. Pope Hadrian I had reacted against Adoptionism as early as 785, but its association with the older, and similar, heresy of Nestorianism convinced the pope that a new synod was necessary. There is considerable debate as to whether Adoptionism was merely a new version of this old error. Nestorianism is the view that the man Christ is *not* to be identified with God the Son. Instead, Christ's human nature is united with the Son who actually lives in him. More than likely, Adoptionism grew out of a distinctly Spanish ecclesiastical culture, and was not of Nestorian inspiration.

Historians disagree as to whether Alcuin had ever been ordained a priest, or even merely as a deacon. He might well have been closely associated with the Benedictine order, but could only have been a member of their secular clergy. Whatever his specific place in the hierarchy of the Catholic priesthood, Alcuin's role cannot be underestimated. In 796, Alcuin was appointed Abbot of St. Martin's at Tours by Charlemagne. After serving Church and king, Alcuin died on 19 May 804.

Context

During Alcuin's years of ministry, Charlemagne implemented a double policy. One was that of armed conquest, by which he gained Visigothic Spain, Lombardian Italy, and much Saxon land. In 774, he had won a major battle over the Lombards, which had opened wide the doors of Italy. In the decades that followed, the Frankish king pursued this military approach. This first policy was often conflated with a religious one, the Christianisation of the new lands. This is the most debatable dimension of Charlemagne's program, and Alcuin, though a great admirer of the king, tried to steer the imperial policy towards the conquered tribes in a more lenient direction.

As a consequence Charlemagne implemented a second aim, which was none other than the union of the Latin and the "barbarian" worlds. Cultural and political unity were essential to maintain peace and order. At the end of the ninth century, with the Muslim armies in possession of most of Spain, Charlemagne's goal could only be achieved if unity in the new faith was part of the new created order. In this context, choosing the Anglo-Saxon Alcuin as an addition to the imperial palace in 781 was a smart choice.

Alcuin's appointment as Master of the Palace School should also be seen as serving Charlemagne's goal of unifying the two European worlds. Through taxation, Charlemagne continued to accumulate a great amount of wealth from the conquered tribes. These riches did not just sit in the government's accounts, but were invested to make the imperial court a centre of learning and culture. The best scholars of the age were attracted to Aachen, where the imperial court was located.

We should not be too naive about Charlemagne's goal, however. If he had a great fascination for learning and "classical" culture, he was also a very perceptive administrator. He knew that in order to rule the vast empire he was building, he would need a proper administration. The Palace School had a very specific goal: it was not learning for its own sake, but the training of highly skilled administrators, clerics, and noblemen, on whom he could rely to preserve the integrity of the empire, and give it a lasting reality. In doing so, Charlemagne's policy wove together Western Europe's intellectual, political, and religious history.

Through the constitution of the Palace School, Alcuin was able to promote the creation of numerous schools of varied levels of learning, through monasteries and cathedrals. To do so, Alcuin had the support of the imperial funds. He used it to procure for the schools books and manuscripts from all over Europe, especially from Britain and Italy. Implementing Charlemagne's policy, Alcuin built a tradition of learning that evolved into the later medieval curriculum known as the Trivium and Quadrivium. What was being created, without Alcuin knowing it, was a Western canon of learning. This was the early foundation of a tradition from which Peter Abelard, Anselm of Canterbury, and Thomas Aquinas would emerge, and through them, the theological method known as scholasticism.

The medieval curriculum would later include foundations of law, theology, literature, language, and moral philosophy, to name but a few. The scope of learning was deep and wide. A global set of skills was an integral part of medieval learning. By contrast, our contemporary age has emphasised specialisation which has led in part to the fragmentation of human knowledge. Economy, literature, and philosophy can now be studied independently without any real relationship being established between disciplines. This can only come at the expense of the ability to see human life as wholly under the guidance of God, which in turn leads to isolating them from the Christian faith.

Faith would have a transformative power only over the spiritual realm, nothing else.

Alcuin's learning was not only used in the context of Charlemagne's growing bureaucracy, but was also used by the Northumbrian to promote unity throughout Western Europe. He tried to do this through reorganising the Latin liturgy in use in the Western church, as well as highlighting the role of liturgical prayers and Christian creeds. In strengthening the unity of the Western church, he inadvertently turned the Eastern Church further away from the West. His defence of the Frankish empire came at the detriment of Western and Eastern dialogue, though we cannot blame Alcuin for the political divide between East and West. In the East, the Emperor at Byzantium continued to hold that he was ultimately the sole authority. This led to the Eastern Church resenting Charlemagne's assumption of the title of Holy Roman Emperor, and inevitably hardened their opposition in doctrinal debates.

Alcuin and Christ's Sonship

During Alcuin's life, at the close of the eighth century, a major controversy erupted. A theological crisis crystallised around a Christological position called "Adoptionism," which was promoted mostly in the Spanish churches. The crisis was complicated by the Adoptionists' claim of simply following the path of pope Leo the Great, and Augustine. Moreover, they added that their language was quite legitimate, already being used in the liturgical language. Christ, who was God himself, "emptied himself, by taking the form of a servant, being born in the likeness of men" (Phil 2:7). Spanish theologians like Elipandus, Archbishop of Toledo, and Felix, Bishop of Urgell, wrestled with the hard question: "What could the apostle mean?" He could first talk about the way God manifested Himself, as divine and human. He could also simply refer to Christ's human nature: Christ was truly made like us. Adoptionists in the Spanish church leaned towards the second option.

To understand the Adoptionists' position, we must go back a little farther in time. Earlier on, Elipandus had reacted to another error that claimed that the three persons of the Trinity were at work in Christ. This resulted, he said, from a lack of understanding of the uniqueness of Christ. Of course, the three persons of the Trinity are always united and always work in unity. An ancient saying affirmed that the visible works of the Trinity are indivisible: the three persons are always at work. Some deduced that in Christ, all three persons were equally at work. If that were the case, however, that would mean that Christ was not uniquely the second person of the Trinity. This, said Elipandus, was a serious error.

A proper understanding of the uniqueness of Christ was absolutely essential. Against this first error, Elipandus affirmed that it was essential to the faith that Christ was "adopted" in His humanity, though not in His divinity. It was important to maintain this because one objective of the mediator was to make us like Him. In order to do that, the person of Christ could only be human in an adoptive manner, thus opening the door to divine adoption for us, His people. If we are sons of God (Rom. 8:14), it is because we are adopted by Him. How could that be? We are adopted because of Christ. In Him, human nature is adopted by God. Christ thus granted the possibility for all who are human to be adopted by God.

There is something profound in what Elipandus is saying here. It is through grace and adoption that we are restored by God and called His children. Christ is the one by whom adoption through grace is possible. We are indeed adopted as sons through Christ the Son. This is a great dimension of our faith confessed in the Westminster Confession of Faith (art. XII):

> All those that are justified, God vouchsafeth, in and for His only Son Jesus Christ, to make partakers of the grace of adoption (Eph 1:5; Gal 4:4-5); by which they are taken into the

number, and enjoy the liberties and privileges of the children
of God (Rom 8:17; Jn 1:12).

Adoption itself is a grace received in Christ (French Confession
of Faith, art. XVII), who is the firstborn of a new people, brother
of the members of a new family formed through adoption.
The fact that He is God the Son does not detract us from this
wonderful truth: that the people of God are an adopted family
through the mediatorial ministry of one who is fully God and
fully man.

Of course, without great care, the language Elipandus used
could be confusing. A line could easily be crossed: adoption
could rapidly become a term used to mean that Christ was *merely*
of human nature adopted to/by the divine. The implication
would be that Christ was not really God. This would be a clear
theological impasse. Would the person called Christ have really
acquired salvation for us? That would mean that He, who was
only of a human nature, could acquire salvation! If that were the
case, why could we not acquire salvation by ourselves, since we
share the same human nature? We can see what is wrong here.
Christ was able to secure salvation because He was the mediator
between God and man, because He was fully God *and* fully man.
We can receive the benefits of redemption and adoption because
the *person* we worship and call Christ acquired them for us.

The Christological discussions in which Elipandus was
engaged led him to contest an affirmation of faith adopted by
the Council of Toledo in 675. There, theologians had searched
the Scriptures and explained that faithful biblical teaching
should recognise Christ as the Son of God by nature, not merely
by adoption. This teaching was opposed by Elipandus, who
enlisted the great mind of Felix of Urgell. They both defended
that a stronger language of adoption was needed to give Christ
His full human nature.

By taking that road, this formulation of Adoptionism was
seen as a new form of Nestorianism. This view of adoption
was rather radical: Christ was only a man adopted by God.

While this clearly goes counter to the testimony of the New Testament, this Adoptionism relied on a certain complexity of language found in the Scriptures. For example, they interpreted Christ's declaration about "not knowing the day or the hour" (Matt. 24:36) as pointing to the existence of the sole human nature of Christ. What was only a demonstration of God's condescension in His incarnation was interpreted more radically as a clear sign that Christ was actually only man—subsequently adopted by God, but not of divine nature. The opponents of Adoptionists thought that this implied that Christ was of a single human nature. That would be a very serious issue because it would render the work of salvation impossible. Human nature in and of itself, cannot achieve salvation.

Felix and Elipandus were trying to avoid the conclusion that Christ was *only* of a human nature, though their view could easily lead them there. We should be careful, however, to not caricature this view, for these Adoptionists accepted the Chalcedonian formulations which talked about Christ as of "one person and two natures". That is why Alcuin promoted the creed of Chalcedon to preserve unity. Of course, there were different ways to understand this expression. Felix and Elipandus distinguished too strictly between the "essential" Son of God and the adopted Son of God. For them, in reference to His divine nature, Christ was truly the only-begotten Son of God (invoking for example John 10:17–18, 14:28), though by adoption He was only the first-begotten Son of God (here relying on Col. 1:8). In doing so, their language seemed to present a "two Christs" perspective.

Elipandus' and Felix's opponents were concerned that their Adoptionist language was used to placate their Muslim overlords. Elipandus was under Muslim Moorish rule, independent from Charlemagne, and thus relatively protected. This gave him some theological freedom vis-à-vis the Frankish Church and even the pope. To use too freely the language of adoption for Christ could be an accommodation to Islam, and its view of Christ not as God, but as one of the great prophets, as a creature of Allah. While that does not appear to be the motivation behind Elipandus' and Felix's formulations, it is easy to see why their opponents could see their theology as too accommodating to Islamic doctrine.

For the Adoptionists' opponents, the mistake of Elipandus and Felix was that they applied the language of Sonship, and thus of adoption, to Christ's *human* nature. To Alcuin, Christ was the Son in His person. Sonship was the true character and identity of the person of Christ, the person of the mediator. To start anywhere else would risk compromising the healthy scriptural balance uniting divine and human natures in one person. Alcuin, and others with him, invoked New Testament passages such as Romans 8:32 and Ephesians 5:2 in support of the Chalcedonian view. They concluded again and again that while Christ is the eternal Son of God, He is at the same time, mysteriously, truly and completely the Son of Man.

In the view of his opponents, Elipandus was making another mistake in associating the virtue of humility only with the human nature. For Alcuin and his allies, Christ becoming the human servant was the direct consequence of His condescension. This was not an *emptying* of the divine attributes, it was the faithful *manifestation* of divine attributes. To miss that was to downplay Christ's role as mediator. His person is the perfect union of human and divine natures, the only embodiment of the divine for human salvation. Christ the Son must be worshipped as the divine Lord who came as a humble servant, whilst never ceasing to be God.

The controversy, however, went beyond that. Some clerics went further, and used a language that was far less cautious. The result was a more direct description of Christ as truly *needing* adoption, symbolised by His baptism, in order to be fully like us. As a human, He needed adoption. As divine, He did not. The problem is that this could result in two "Christs", one that was truly human, and the other one who, fully God, could be human in name only. Alcuin answered by maintaining the credal Christological expression: God the Son is one person, the only-begotten Son of God, existing in two natures, human and divine.

This formulation was probably not fully satisfying. It does not explain everything. To Alcuin, this was not an issue, however, because there is mystery in the person of the mediator. Alcuin warns us to beware of our rationalist tendency to accept and confess only what can be fully explained through human reason. Christ could not be adopted in His divine nature: He had always been the Son of God, that is who He is. Therefore, when talking about adoption with respect to Christ, it could be only in reference to His human nature. Christ's human nature was adopted by God. That was the rationalistic reasoning of these Adoptionists.

Alcuin teaches us something vital about our faith, and the manner in which we approach Scripture. We should always take biblical teaching in its entirety. These Adoptionists erred because they relied too exclusively on passages that could be interpreted to confirm their position. They attempted to explain the mystery of Christ's two natures in a manner that seemed quite easy to understand. It was, however, also too rational. It tried to separate too easily terms that should be used only with respect to either the human or to the divine nature of Christ. Given that the incarnation is the "mystery of godliness" (1 Tim. 3:16), maybe such a goal was unrealistic, unwise, and even too much at odds with the witness of Scripture. We must maintain a healthy view of the limits of reason, or we will be tempted by a rational tendency which will lead us away from the mystery of the incarnation. Instead of being led to worship, we will be led to purely intellectual formulations.

Felix of Urgell was summoned by Charlemagne in 791 and his teaching condemned in 792, though he succeeded in returning to Spain the same year, seeking refuge with Elipandus. The Bishop of Toledo took steps to defend the Spanish position, arguing in a letter that the Frankish church had constantly downplayed the state of humiliation of the Son. Following this letter, Alcuin was called back from his homeland, where he was on a mission for Charlemagne. To resolve the issue, Alcuin exhorted Felix and Elipandus to submit to the political ruler and to use the Nicene creed in the liturgy, since the creed was confessed by both Spanish and Frankish churches. In doing so, Alcuin was trying to preserve the integrity of Charlemagne's empire, while promoting unity through spirituality.

Alcuin's example shows us that even when we think we are defending biblical and orthodox teaching, we should strive to promote unity. We have often forgotten the value of liturgical prayers. The use of ecumenical creeds has slowly disappeared from the life of the Church to its great impoverishment and to the detriment of promoting and manifesting Christian unity. This does not mean we will automatically agree on the meaning of our confessions, but it will provide a theological basis for further discussion.

Conclusion

The Adoptionist crisis in which Alcuin took part was not the most important part of his life and work, but it provides great lessons for us. It requires that we read God's Word in its entirety, that we weigh and take into account the whole history of redemption. Alcuin also reminds us that when talking about Christ, we are considering one of the most profound mysteries. It is not something about which nothing can be said, but we should speak with caution about what is revealed. As a gift from the God who speaks, this "mystery of godliness" humbles us by restraining the claims of our reason. Finally, Alcuin teaches us the value of credal affirmation that helps promote Christian unity. In an age of individualised faith, there is great value in listening to the voice of Charlemagne's educator and counsellor.

Gottschalk (814-868)
Divine grace above human works

Biographical sketch

Born into a noble Saxon family around 814, Gottschalk grew up in the monastery of Fulda in Saxony after being offered as a child oblate, i.e. a child dedicated by his parents to become a monk. Fulda was an important centre of learning and education, especially from 803 onwards, when Rabanus became the director of its school. Gottschalk's relationship with him was tense. It came to a head in 829 at the Assembly of Worms, when Gottschalk brought serious charges against his abbot. The young monk argued that he had been tonsured against his will, and coerced to take the vows of monastic life. The situation was aggravated by the fact that Gottschalk, as a nobleman, was defended by his family.

Rabanus, for his part, composed several treatises in which he strongly indicated that the problem with Gottschalk was primarily one of obedience due to a teacher by his pupil. This was a telling example of social disintegration that, for him, threatened the Carolingian Empire. Only after this first stage did the controversy take a definitive doctrinal and personal dimension. Rabanus argued that, in opposing his superiors, Gottschalk was adopting the ways of "heretics" and "schismatics", thus reverting to the pagan world he was supposed to have left behind. Rabanus also argued that the Saxons' conversion was too recent for them to have already learned the value of true Christian life. Their duty was obedience to their spiritual counsellors, not opposition to authority. The result of this assembly was that Gottschalk's inheritance was restored to his family, and in return he fully embraced his monastic vows.

The 830s saw Gottschalk at the monastery of Corbie, in northern France, from where a renewed missionary work in Scandinavia was launched. Around 836, he left Corbie to journey to Italy where, according to the numerous enemies he had already made, he began to spread dangerous teachings on the subject of predestination. It is certain that Gottschalk's teaching on predestination intensified during the 830s. During the decade 836-846, Gottschalk engaged in heated debates with local Italian bishops, even opposing the influential bishop of Verona, who in turn requested from Rabanus a theological treatise to answer Gottschalk's errors.

Around 846, he was forced to leave Italy. It seems that he was either expelled due to the contentious nature of his teaching, or that he decided to leave in order to further the cause of Christ— and of his political protector Eberhard, Duke of Frioul (Trieste, Venice). About the same time, Rabanus composed a lengthy letter to the same Eberhard. Rabanus painted Gottschalk as a heretic and charlatan, along with all those who accepted his teaching. Between 846 and 848 Gottschalk preached through Dalmatia (an area covering much of Croatia, Bosnia and Herzegovina, Montenegro, Kosovo and Serbia) and Pannonia (Vienna, Budapest). This choice was the consequence of a strategic decision to extend the popularity of his preaching, with the support of Eberhard. In doing so, Gottschalk was undertaking an evangelistic endeavour that had great political significance. Whatever his faults, he was recognised as a charismatic preacher.

During that time, Eberhard chose to distance himself from the perceived heretical teaching of his protégé. Gottschalk's ecclesiastical hierarchy soon summoned him to appear at the Synod of Mainz (848), presided over by Louis the German, one of the grandsons of Charlemagne. Rabanus, who was also part of the synod, was by then an archbishop seen as a force for the purification of the Church through the denunciation of heretics and pseudo-prophets. This explains his uncompromising opposition to Gottschalk in 848: the purity of the Church was at stake. The problem was that Gottschalk also presented himself as defender of the Church's purity against the errors of his former superior. At the Synod of Mainz, Gottschalk presented a confession of faith before the bishops in which he openly defended his belief in double predestination, and more crucially, its necessity. Gottschalk affirmed that God predestined, willed, some to be saved, and some to be damned, in the exact same manner. In arguing in this manner, he seemed to disconnect one's status as "lost" from one's status as a sinner before God.

After witnessing Gottschalk's refusal to change his beliefs, Rabanus encouraged the synod to send Gottschalk to Orbais to be under the guard of Hincmar, Archbishop of Reims, who was already a ferocious critic of the Saxon monk. The synod ruled accordingly, assigning the recalcitrant monk to what was effectively "house arrest" in the monastery. In his larger confession of faith, written during his "imprisonment" at Orbais, Gottschalk presents himself as divinely inspired. In this work, he exhorts his readers to accept the truth of his teaching and to accept his doctrine of double predestination. In his view, this doctrine was increasingly used as a sign of someone's status as one of the elect, and less as confidence in one's redemption by God.

Six months later, the Synod of Quierzy (849) confirmed the ruling of the Synod of Mainz. Gottschalk was publicly flogged and imprisoned at Hautvillers, where he spent the rest of his days until his death in 868. Gottschalk managed to send treatises and letters to many influential people, arousing public interest in his case. The monks at Hautvillers were influenced by his teaching and by his perseverance in the face of persecution. Gottschalk remained defiant, winning support from within the walls of the monastery. Rothad, the great bishop of Soissons, another enemy of Hincmar, did nothing to restrain Gottschalk's activities.

A few years later, in 853, a new synod met at Quierzy in order to put an end to the predestinarian controversy. Hincmar succeeded in having the synod adopt four articles that, while they did not address Gottschalk directly, were nonetheless a condemnation of his teaching. These articles are worth mentioning: first, there is only one predestination and no one is predestined to punishment; second, free will is restored through grace at baptism; third, God's will is that all be saved, though not all will be; fourth, Christ's blood is shed for all, but not all are saved. This new ruling did not stop Gottschalk from expressing his strong opposition to all who opposed his doctrine of double predestination. His literary activity was facilitated by some of Hautvillers' monks who had sympathy for his struggle against the debatable attitude of their hierarchy.

The formal end of the controversy took place in 860 at the Synod of Tusey, which confirmed the following: first, that there was indeed predestination to salvation; second, that grace *and* free will were necessary for salvation; third, the synod kept silent on the issue of predestination to damnation. While Gottschalk's specific teachings were not officially reported (there is no formal rejection of his version of double predestination), these final rulings were an implicit condemnation of Gottschalk. But this again did not stop Gottschalk's teaching from spreading during the final decade of his life.

Gottschalk died on October 30 of a year unknown, thought to be 868. Even on his deathbed, he found the energy, and disdain, necessary to repudiate Hincmar's last effort to extract a retraction out of the dying monk.

Socio-political and theological context

The first half of the century was a time of intense transformation. Charlemagne's empire would soon be divided amongst his three grandsons, and the integration of pagan Saxon tribes into a new political unity was still a work in progress. After Charlemagne, the Carolingian focus on religious harmony, unity, and orthodoxy came to be even more crucial amidst the turbulent dynastic conflicts and political fragmentation of the ninth century. Many social institutions and rituals participated in this production of unity in the midst of disorder. The dedication of children to the religious life was one way of cementing the participation of the pagan tribes in the "Christian" empire.

In many ways, this socio-political project motivated the Church's renewed struggle against heretics. If society were to be unified, it could only be so if the Church, for her part, did her best to protect orthodoxy and punish those identified as heretics. This became even more important during the 840s and 850s when medieval France was the stage of a prolonged and vehement debate about the nature of divine grace and double predestination—a debate in which Gottschalk was one of the main actors. As such, and because of his public rejection of superior authority, Gottschalk was the typical heretic of the ninth century.

Labelling Gottschalk a "heretic" was not without difficulty. The use of this notion demanded a proper ecclesiastical discipline in order to maintain the Carolingians' ideal of social unity. Unfortunately, the Carolingian concept of heresy lacked a precise definition. It remained a rather fluid and ambiguous term that was more often used by theological antagonists as a mere derogatory name for their opponents. There was not necessarily any need to interact seriously with the "heretics" before accusing them of departing from the western Catholic orthodoxy which was supposed to be the foundation for Frankish unity. This, of course, is still a strategy often used today. A real or perceived fault, taken by some to be a very serious one, is deemed a "heresy". This fault is not always biblical or theological. It can also be social or political. The heretics rapidly become betrayers and enemies of Christ. To oppose them is to take up the cause of Christ. This process does not accept ambiguity in doctrine or ethics. Everything is so clear and evident that engagement with the opponent's argument is unnecessary.

Seen in this context, Gottschalk's doctrine struck to the heart of the socio-ecclesiastical unity. In defending the absolute priority and effectiveness of God's grace in salvation, he denied human free will and the possibility of doing good works without God. The positive value of grace, faith, and works was reserved for those in whom God had Himself begun His restoring work: the elect. The rest of humankind could not possibly participate in these good works. The implication was clear: the imperial Church could not offer salvation to all, much less promise that it could provide the necessary means to attain salvation. This could only affect the Carolingian effort to build a cohesive society.

In reaction, the Synod of Paris (829) affirmed that Christian faith without good works was not enough for salvation. The synergy between man and God was absolutely necessary. For Gottschalk, on the contrary, humility, repentance, and faith, were the only requirements to receive saving grace. There again, free will was impotent without the antecedent work of God's grace. This negatively affected the core of the daily practice of faith: penance served as the principal means through which reconciliation between God and each other was possible. The active practice of penance did not merely serve a theological purpose but also a social one.

When the penitent was restored to the Christian community he was *de facto* restored to the human society. What if the so-called penitent could not really be considered able to practice good works because he was not judged to be one of the "elect"? That was highly problematic considering the social and moral reform undertaken in the Frankish world. How could such a "morally reformed" society be built, if the members of the said society could not practice good works? It could not. Gottschalk held that not all individuals in the empire could achieve salvation, or do good works.

The difficulty for the Carolingian empire to present itself as the protector against the perverting influence of heretics worsened when Gottschalk and his supporters turned this on its head. They were the real guardians of the Church's doctrinal purity, against the errors of their ecclesiastical hierarchy. Even the imperial Church could be heretical. The coercive reform favoured by the Carolingian Church, in contrast to outright persecution, was not a sure sign of it being a guardian of orthodoxy.

The ninth century was also a time when heresies, of the kind the Church had dealt with during the Fourth and Fifth Centuries, were for many people a thing of the past. The term "heretic", while it was often reserved for foreigners who departed from orthodoxy, was rarely applied to Carolingian monks or bishops. The word "heretic" was applied to outsiders, and this played into the hands of a world trying to transform itself into the guarantor of social unity.

This did not mean that "heresy" disappeared from the Church's life and theology. Without strict and direct reference to what being a heretic actually was, the term came to be used to disparage one's opponent. Gottschalk did not hesitate to describe the bishops opposing him as heretics who endangered the integrity of the Church, acting as wolves instead of shepherds. His opponents, in particular Rabanus and Hincmar, returned the favour, presenting Gottschalk under the guise of the great deceiver, not only as a heretic, but an agent of the devil sent to lead simple believers astray. Both parties were engaged in something typical of the Carolingian world.

Carolingian clerics who participated in this debate tried to define heresy in their own terms to suit their own conclusions. They carefully selected their sources in a manner that reflected their theology, representing patristic tradition to their own advantage. Gottschalk, as well as Rabanus and Hincmar, adopted this pattern of self-justification. Gottschalk assumed the position of defender of the ecclesiastical tradition through his selection of patristic authorities, including Augustine, Gregory the Great, and Isidore of Seville. To reinforce the legitimacy of his teaching, he did not hesitate to pass over the works of the same authors that presented a more nuanced view.

Gottschalk's participation in the predestinarian debate was facilitated by the ambiguity of the Church's own teaching on the matter. Between the times of Augustine and Gottschalk, the ecclesiastical hierarchy of the Western churches did not bind their clerics to a precise view of predestination. Following the debates over free will in the century, a variety of views coexisted. The Catholic world included a strict Augustinian position—for which predestination is seen as an eternal decree saving the elect—as well as a more moderate, semi-Augustinian one—which instead stressed mere divine foreknowledge of human choices. Man's exercise of free will, before the reception of saving grace, was often affirmed. It is clear from Gottschalk's historical context, that a significant number of the Carolingian bishops held to something very close to the latter view.

Moreover, these contrasting views were often found in the same treatise. Both Pelagian and Augustinian perspectives were at times amalgamated, without a clear coherent theology being formulated. Proof-texting one's teaching was made easy. This does not necessarily invalidate a given conclusion, though it begs the question of the means adopted to defend a biblical doctrine. Gottschalk was a theologian of his times. This does not justify the debatable methods he adopted, but that could serve as a warning for all those engaged in the task of "doing" theology—which is, in the end, dialogue with the living God.

Whenever we prepare a sermon, talk with another believer (or non-believer), or just read the Scriptures, we should be careful about our attitudes. The study of God's Word should not only be an exercise in doctrinal purity. It is also an exercise in personal transformation. Or rather, our exercise in doctrinal purity should include the humility of the Christian life, and the renewal of our attitudes through the fruits of the Spirit. Our attitude can work in favour of, or against, our theology. Gottschalk's ministry is a clear example.

Theology

Gottschalk of Orbais is often seen as one who stood virtually alone in promoting the sovereignty of God in a time when Semi-Pelagian soteriology ruled supreme. This superficial perspective is reinforced by the lack of a coherent and systematic account of the whole of Gottschalk's teaching on double predestination and grace. Moreover, there is a temptation to read into Gottschalk's works meanings he never intended. We are tempted to "reconstruct" the rebellious Saxon's original teaching, at the risk of importing questions and debates that did not belong to his time into his theology.

The debate over predestination, especially double predestination, can be framed in very different ways. The seventeenth century Protestant debate over predestination and Christ's efficacious work cannot be simply imported into the ninth-century debate which was concerned, maybe more than anything, with the validity of free will. Moreover, the later Protestant debates infused a new vocabulary into this millennial debate. The theological vocabulary of predestination has grown richer and richer during the seven centuries that separate Gottschalk and Arminius. Thus, extreme caution is needed to avoid anachronisms.

The controversy of which Gottschalk was part is often described as predestinarian in nature, and it is. But it is as much a debate about the priority of divine grace with respect to salvation. Gottschalk argued that God had chosen some individuals for eternal life and others for eternal damnation, a position he argued was entirely orthodox according to western Catholic tradition. Of course, he also argued that it was the only possible orthodox reading both of Scripture and of the Church Fathers, which is debatable.

Before trying to present the main thrust of Gottschalk's argument for divine grace, we should note that Gottschalk's theology contained apparent ambiguities that his detractors were more than willing to use against him. For example, in a letter sent to a certain "Bishop Lupus," written during his time in Italy, Gottschalk described grace as the sole means of receiving salvation. This seems to be consistent with his vehemently proclaimed priority of divine grace. At the same time, he granted that the intercession of the "elect" (in this case, that of "Bishop Lupus") could help bring this about. The intercession of the believers' prayers, as well as their merits, had a real and concrete role to play, and were not completely insignificant.

Gottschalk's reader could be perplexed: divine grace was the sole means of salvation, though intercession by bishop and saints was not irrelevant. Of course, the paradox is only apparent. The great Augustine of Hippo had already pointed out that God ordains the means for the reception of grace. If God ordains the prayers of the believers as a means for grace, then there is no opposition between the priority of grace and the role of those prayers. Of course, this does not imply that this view is the most biblical. It only means that Gottschalk's theology was not necessarily confronted with an irreconcilable tension on that issue.

A few essential traits of Gottschalk's theology can now be presented. To begin with, God's predestination concerns every person, and is directed at their final state. Thus, it makes no sense to speak only about predestination to life. God's action is one. Thus, if He elected some to life, He elected others to death. Predestination is for Him necessarily twofold. The important question is whether there is a strict parallel between these two sides of predestination. Gottschalk, it seems, would argue for a real symmetry. The Scriptures, however, maintain a healthy distinction between the two sides to predestination. It is possible to maintain that God is sovereign in all His decrees and in everything, whilst also recognising that election and damnation are asymmetrical in motivation and in operation. God's action towards salvation is not symmetrical to His passing over those who are left in their sin.

As for the reason for election, Gottschalk teaches that predestination to eternal death is made on the basis of the foreknowledge of their "evil merits". In a similar manner, God, who knows everything and cannot be deceived, simultaneously and permanently decreed beforehand to bestow grace and life on some, but not on others. Only then could God be completely just in the operation of grace and judgement. Anything else would open the door to God being arbitrary, and render Him dependent upon a human work of acceptance or rejection of His grace.

If Gottschalk had been satisfied with this, he might not have erred as much as he did. Asked whether God wanted all people to be saved, he answered negatively. Gottschalk did not explain in detail why it was the case, probably because the conclusion was obvious to him. If God really desired to save all, all would be saved. If some are not saved, it is because God does not want them to be saved. It follows logically, for Gottschalk, that Christ died only to redeem the elect. For him, Christ gave His life to unite His people, thus, only the elect benefit from His death. Moreover, to say that Christ accomplished salvation for all, but that some will not be saved, is in effect to say that some part of Christ's work was not sufficient since some could resist it. But to Gottschalk, Christ could not have given His body and blood in vain. Here, he uses something typical of his theological method: a strict and simple syllogism. Such a way of theologising was done at the expense of the richness of the biblical language. It is impossible to reduce the unfathomable motivation of the eternal and infinite God to a few sets of logical statements.

In his teaching on grace and election, Gottschalk answered what he perceived to be a serious theological error, something that had been considered a heresy. In his mind, he defended the orthodox position against a form of Pelagianism, whereby man's free will was more or less preserved. Gottschalk defended that since humans can only do evil after the Fall, only God's grace can restore their will. No human will was free from sin.

Through His free and gracious gift, God renders His elect able to participate in the good works He has prepared for them. The reprobate do not share in that grace, and thus they cannot do good works, nor can they properly distinguish between good and evil. They remain completely lost and have no positive ability in themselves.

Gottschalk's teaching was also motivated by his opponents' view of baptism. Hincmar, like Rabanus, taught that the grace received at baptism renewed free will, and that thus all baptised alike could practice good works, apart from explicit faith. Gottschalk denied that baptism could have such a positive effect without the previous restoring work of God's saving grace. Baptism was, in effect, of no use for the reprobate. In the same way, if someone who is not elect received the Eucharist, the body and blood of Christ were of no help for salvation since the latter is received by faith and precedes participation in the sacraments. The sacraments are God's remedy for our daily sufferings, and this divine nourishment is of no value to those who are not previously saved.

The uniting conviction throughout these teachings is the absolute priority of God's grace toward salvation. Gottschalk was uncompromising regarding the necessity of grace, to the point of aggression and divisiveness. It is the unchanging nature and work of the creating, redeeming, and restoring triune God that is at the centre of the monk's teaching. Gottschalk always stressed the unlimited grace of God over human actions. For him, it was a heresy to give a place to human action and will that could threaten the priority of God's free grace. This was not just a matter of doctrine, but a matter of the salvation of souls. God is always the active agent in salvation. The elects' free will has no part in it: Gottschalk rather stresses that the elect's position is that of a thankful recipient of God's grace. There was a deep pastoral concern to his stress on the priority of grace manifested in double predestination.

In response to Gottschalk's teaching, Rabanus wrote a treatise on predestination in which he showed that not only was Gottschalk erring in his theological opinion, but he was also taking interest in matters that were irrelevant. In fact, the question of predestination of the elect was not an important issue because grace received through baptism made salvation possible for believers. The only thing needed was cooperation through good works based on the exercise of free will. Salvation would only be "visible" in the future when perpetual reward would be gained through the actions of free-will directed at good works.

Focus and relevance

Gottschalk, despite his emphasis on the priority of faith in the gift of salvation, was not a perfect teacher. In his later writings on predestination, he exhibits a tenacity that borders on aggression. He encourages his reader to debate with whomever opposes his doctrine. Whatever else we might think about his formulation concerning double predestination, the tone he adopted in this latest stage of the controversy pushes the readers to defend Gottschalk, no matter the cost, and no matter what else Scripture might be teaching.

We should beware of presenting Gottschalk's overall teaching as an unambiguous formulation of biblical purity against the theological corruption of his opponents. The situation is often much more complex. And so it is with Gottschalk. For example, his very rational form of theologising could lead him to downplay other essential aspects of Scripture's teaching, like the diversity of God's expressions of love. Gottschalk also had the tendency, later in his writings, to identify the elect with the acceptance of double predestination, which clearly goes beyond sound and balanced biblical doctrine.

Further, his style of argumentation could be re-evaluated. Gottschalk made extensive use of syllogism to overwhelm his opponent with questions so as to demonstrate the superiority of his own "Christian" argument. He constructed his reasoning as a three-part argument: first he started with a passage of Scripture, second he moved on to a quotation of the Church Fathers or his own analysis; third, he concluded with a strong assertion of sound doctrine.

Gottschalk found precedence in this syllogistic practice both in the Apostle Paul's letter to the Galatians (in particular), as well as in great Church Fathers like Augustine and Jerome. For example, he held that it is logical that God should not will all men to be saved: if God willed to save all men, all men would be saved, since God is omnipotent; because Scriptures bear witness that not all will be saved, and since God is indeed omnipotent, God does not will to save all men. Unfortunately, his formulation is over-rational. Gottschalk is trying to explain completely, in ways accessible to human reason, the inner workings of God's decree of salvation. His approach is a cautionary tale: we should respect the limits of our reason and proceed with prudence when explaining what God has done from eternity past.

Gottschalk does indeed explore election in a manner that is overly rational, even unbalanced. We should not be too quick to pass judgement on Gottschalk. We are still in the early stages of defining a more precise theology of predestination. Gottschalk is trying to formulate a theology of God's decree but he does so without the privilege that we have: twelve centuries have passed since Gottschalk, and we have the benefit of so much theological wisdom! Gottschalk did not have the support of centuries of Christian theology. He is writing seven hundred years before Luther and he lacks nuance, but we should not expect too much. That helps us read him with charity: his theology is an early affirmation of salvation by faith alone, due to God's gracious and sovereign decree, even though his formulation is less nuanced and rich than that of the Reformers.

We could object rightly to many aspects of Gottschalk's presentation of double predestination. One mistake would be to see him only through dogmatic eyes, forgetting that he is a historical figure. We tend to evaluate his view of predestination through the lens of our own theological tradition. We should not forget that Luther comes seven hundred years after him, and the Westminster Confession of Faith, eight hundred years. It is true that the Reformers' teaching on predestination is more balanced than Gottschalk's and that they tend to stress the asymmetrical nature of predestination. Though there is election and damnation, they do not operate in an identical manner. This is true enough, but theology is also an historical endeavour that has been enriched through the centuries, with more precision and distinctions being added. We should be careful before evaluating Gottschalk in the light of all that we have gained in the five hundred years since the Reformation. We should cast a humble and generous eye on Gottschalk. In five hundred years, we might well need our theological descendants to be as generous with us.

Gottschalk's teaching on predestination serves as a dual reminder. First, double predestination has a long theological history, but can also be construed in very different ways. Not every theologian and believer who holds, in varying degree, to double predestination would stand with Gottschalk, especially with his method of presentation. Second, we should hear Augustine's warning about the certainty of knowledge of one's predestined state, a warning that Gottschalk was too quick to forget. In fact, Gottschalk erred in his affirmation that certainty as to the individual's status as elect could be ascertained on the basis of their acceptance of the doctrine of double predestination. Gottschalk's attitude betrays a certain lack of humility, compassion, and love. While he demonstrated a genuine compassion for those not in Christ's fold, he was overly rigid with those who entertained doubts about his own theology. This should lead us to think more deeply about how to distinguish between essential and secondary, even tertiary, doctrines. Gottschalk could not make such distinctions, and it affected his defence of the much-needed centrality and priority of divine grace.

Predestination, taken first and foremost as a confession of God's activity prior to any activity on man's part, was not a doctrine that had been lost in the Early Middle Ages, only to be rediscovered by Gottschalk in the mid-ninth century. Even double predestination, so dear to the Saxon monk, was not completely foreign to the previous centuries. Gottschalk was not an isolated voice in the midst of a medieval wilderness, though he faced great opposition. This opposition should not be taken as a rejection of the necessity of grace, or even as a rejection of "simple" predestination.

The heart of Gottschalk's teaching was the absolute priority of God's grace. While this could seem obvious, it is too easy to forget. Loyalty to our own traditions, overconfidence in our own works, or desire for self-validation, and a desire to conform to the ecclesiastical or social world, can threaten the role of divine grace. This fundamental point should always be brought back to us, again and again, so as to remind us that God alone, in Christ, is the author and perfecter of our faith (Heb. 12:2).

Conclusion

Gottschalk is a good example of how the desire to teach and promote a healthy and biblical theology can lead to serious imbalance. He never ceased to show that God was never purely passive and that God's will was always somewhat active in reprobation. He reminded us that God is the one ultimately in control and nothing escapes His sovereignty. He opposed an extreme attitude, which would leave humans masters of their fate. Unfortunately, Gottschalk went a step further and did not differentiate the action of God's will in election or reprobation. That was his great fault. For him, God's action was always identical in motivation. In doing so, he erred on the side of rationalising predestination, not only in defending a "double predestination" which stresses that God is sovereign in election and damnation, but further arguing for a symmetrical operation of both.

Gottschalk had no room for the biblical balance displayed in either the Westminster Confession of Faith (§10) or the Gallican Confession (§12). In both of these Reformed confessions, God actively seeks out the elect, out of sheer grace and love. The deliberate "active action" on God's part is not paralleled in reprobation which is merely a "passive action," or a bypassing of the reprobate. God leaves those who are not elect in their unbelief through the hardening of hearts. In a great example of scriptural balance, both confessions are content to dwell on God's wonderful action on behalf of sinners. This leads us to worship God and nourishes our compassion for those who, from our perspective, have not yet been embraced by Christ.

Gottschalk rightly opposed one mistake of his day, one that gave human will too much freedom to do what is good in the eyes of God. As is often the case, when one opposes an error, one is tempted to overcompensate. That is what happened with Gottschalk, and it should be a warning for us. His teaching and ministry remind us that we should always beware of our tendency to construe a theological system that leaves no room for the mystery of God. We should always let the Scriptures model our theology. God's Word should continue to speak to us, always and in everything.

Anselm of Canterbury (1033–1109)

Defender of the Incarnation

Biographical sketch

Anselm was born in 1033 in Aosta, Italy. His father, Gundulf, was a Lombard who had become a citizen of Aosta, but saw the fortunes of his family decline at the turn of the century. Anselm's childhood was marked by two things: first Anselm could feel the presence of God deeply impressed on him and all around him from a young age, to the point that the young child could not conceive of anybody not believing in God. Second, Anselm suffered from a strained relationship with his father, which seems to have affected the bond between them. Such was not the case with his mother. Unfortunately, the death of his mother in 1056, and the growing estrangement between himself and his father, led the young man to leave Aosta, fleeing an uncertain future as well as a discontented life.

There is no doubt that, with his sudden "escape," Anselm walked right into the unknown. Neither the monastic vocation, nor a moderately successful political office were an option—at least at that moment of his life. Where did Anselm go? He could have gone different ways, including trying to find his father's Italian family, but he chose instead to look towards the members of his mother's family, who lived in the area of Lyon and Vienne. He spent nearly three years in the Duchy of Burgundy where the monastery of Cluny and other major schools, were located. He also spent time in the kingdom of France. Anselm still did not know what he desired, though he was still haunted by a deep yearning for the religious life, as well as being pulled by the life of the mind. Then, in 1059, he found his way to the Abbey of Le Bec, which was under the leadership of Lanfranc, its increasingly famous prior.

There, Anselm immersed himself in the intellectual and spiritual discipline of the abbey's training. A pressing issue soon presented itself: Anselm could choose one of several paths. He could become a monk or a hermit, or become involved in works of charity, working or running a "hospital". Anselm did not know which way God was leading him, but desired to act according to His will. This spiritual anxiety led him to seek the advice of Lanfranc, who referred the matter to the Archbishop of Rouen. It was decided that the best path for the young man was the monastic life: Anselm would become a novice.

Life at Le Bec was initially difficult for the young novice. His slow "conversion", as he called it, gradually led him to embrace the Benedictine rule. Once he did, there was no turning back for Anselm. Submitting fully to the guidance of the Rule, he at the same time accepted the authority of Lanfranc, prior of the abbey, that is, the second most important figure after the abbot. For Anselm, Le Bec was more or less equated with Lanfranc, teacher of the liberal arts, and one of the great theologians of his age.

His life as a simple monk lasted only for three years, for in 1063 Lanfranc was appointed Abbot of the Abbey of Saint-Etienne, in Caen. Though the office had become vacant, nobody thought Anselm would succeed Lanfranc as prior of Le Bec, since other monks had seniority over him. His election, though, did not provoke anger or resentment: Anselm's care and guidance had won their respect and obedience. In 1078, following the death of Herluin, founder and first Abbot of the abbey of Le Bec, Anselm was quite naturally elected to become the new abbot. This time there was no reticence on the part of the other monks but the newly appointed abbot was hesitant to accept his appointment to the new office. During his time in

Le Bec, Anselm wrote some of his major works, including the *Monologion* and the *Proslogion*, made famous for his formulation of the "ontological argument" for the existence of God. He also had the theological energy to write several dialogues.

Lanfranc became Archbishop of Canterbury in 1070 and when he died in 1089, leaving the great English See vacant, Anselm's life was to change dramatically. The English king William II kept the position empty for four long years, ensuring that its revenues would be kept for the crown. This left the English Church in disarray and without leadership. With the approval of the king, Anselm came to England in 1092, but William II was not ready to proceed with his confirmation. Then, in early 1093, the king fell seriously ill. Moved to repentance on his sick bed he yielded to the exhortation of the nobles and clerics, and confirmed Anselm's election to the archbishopric.

This time it was Anselm who showed some reluctance in accepting this call. His concern was that it would look like he had been aspiring to the office of Canterbury: everything in his humble demeanour shrank away from the suggestion. Some of the very nobles that had convinced William II to recognise his election also convinced Anselm to accept the position, rather forcefully. Anselm was dragged to William's bedside, and there, was confirmed by the king. Anselm then received the confirmation in front of the altar in Canterbury.

As his condition soon improved, the king's consent to Anselm's election weakened. After all, the king had granted church lands to some of his political allies. He could not easily go back on his word. After many mediating efforts on the part of nobles and clerics, Anselm was finally consecrated Archbishop of Canterbury on 4 December 1093. He ought to have been confirmed by Rome, but two candidates claimed to be pope at this time. William decided, because it also suited his purpose, that Anselm should receive no confirmation until the king had taken a position on who was rightfully the pope. Again, Anselm would not be forced into a corner by the king and, at a royal council in 1095, he spoke in support of pope Urban.

The last sign necessary before Anselm could be fully recognised and accepted as Archbishop of Canterbury was to receive the official symbol of his charge. A papal representative brought the pallium, a liturgical vestment, which the king insisted Anselm receive from his hand to assert royal supremacy over the Church. Inevitably, Anselm refused, though a compromise was found: the pallium would be presented on the altar, from which Anselm would take his official symbol.

This final compromise did not heal the divide between the king and the archbishop. On the contrary, William tried to restrain and control Anselm's authority, especially when it came to Church reforms. William also demanded Anselm's support in his struggle against Wales, but the Archbishop was reluctant to give his blessing. Finally, Anselm saw no other option but to seek the advice of the pope. William denied Anselm permission to leave the kingdom. When Anselm nonetheless departed in 1097, he was effectively in exile. During this troubled time, Anselm produced one of his most enduring works, *Cur deus homo?*, written between 1095 and 1098.

In October 1098, pope Urban held a council at Bari, where, among other things, Anselm's case was presented. This council would actually have excommunicated William but for Anselm interceding in favour of the king. While staying in the neighbourhood of Lyon, the news of William's death reached Anselm. The new king, Henry I, summoned him back to England. His return, however, quickly took an air of *déja vu*. Henry required Anselm to receive a new investiture as Archbishop of Canterbury from his royal hand. This would demonstrate his absolute royal authority. Anselm, however, would not be coerced. He responded to the king that the decrees of the Church did not leave him free to choose his course of action. He could not receive the investiture from the king.

Henry decided to seek resolution from the pope, asking for a special exemption, but this request was denied by pope Paschal. After several fruitless envoys to the pope, and seeing that the Bishop of Rome would not change his mind, Henry decided to take a radical step and send Anselm to Rome in 1103. On the continent, Anselm received a letter from the king forbidding him to return. In answer, the pope excommunicated all the English prelates who had accepted consecration from the king, though Henry himself was not excommunicated. Though that was a clear sign addressed to Henry, Anselm was still in exile, and would remain so for four years. It was only when the London Council was held in 1107 that a solution was found: the king would relinquish his claim to have the right to invest clerics, while the Church would allow the said clerics to pay homage for their temporal possessions.

Anselm was allowed to end his two remaining years in relative peace. He continued his pastoral labours and wrote the last of his works, including a treatise on predestination and grace. He died in 1109, in Canterbury, where he is buried.

Social and historical background

A first contextual dimension is the relation between Church and empire, which was often tense in the eleventh century. Anselm's primary context was the antagonism between the temporal powers following the Norman conquest and the Papacy with its socio-cultural acquisitions. Anselm lived in a transitional world. His was the age of pope Gregory VII and William the Conqueror, an age that was wavering between conservatism and innovation. Societies and the political order were changing. Anselm remained strangely unaware of these evolutions, and was even passive regarding the changes. In many ways, he does not seem to have sought to affect the world. His will was not of a political nature. Anselm, however, had a profound impact on the world around him, maybe even a more determinant influence than either pope Gregory VII, or the great William, despite the significant abilities of these men.

While William had a great perception of the secular world, Gregory was a man of purpose and vision for the Church as being independent from the temporal and kingly powers. Anselm, for his part, participated only indirectly in the political and ecclesiastical tensions. The Abbey of Le Bec became the centre of political affairs, involving Duke William of Normandy (William the Conqueror) and pope Nicholas II. When pope Nicholas II sought a new alliance, turning away from the Holy Roman Empire, he looked to the Normans in his hope for a stable and peaceful society. This overture even led to a meeting between Nicholas II and Lanfranc, raising the profile of the Abbey. As a result, the pope would support the Norman invasion of England in 1066. This would lead Lanfranc to Caen, and then to Canterbury. This would also affect Anselm during his tenure as Archbishop of Canterbury.

A second element that serves to highlight the times in which Anselm lived was his "feudalism". This term is ordinarily used to refer to the ordering of society through a clear set of social obligations—among which honour and obedience stand out. In such a model the most vital part of the social order was the relationship between vassal and lord, all obedience being due by the former to the latter. This would explain Anselm's indebtedness to the context of his time, via the notion of honour, and the supposed representation of God as a medieval lord.

This view of the feudal organisation of medieval society has been largely contested. In-depth studies of that age have led scholars to stress the diversity of social realities in the medieval age. It would thus be a tragic mistake to characterise all European societies in exactly the same way. This is a warning to all of us. We tend to use broad categories to facilitate the dismissal of the things we want to see overthrown and abolished. That does not mean that social relationships were not regulated during the medieval ages, but that it is difficult to ascertain to what degree social contexts impacted Anselm's theology.

A third significant contextual element is Anselm's monasticism. As a Benedictine, he lived in a world of order, honour, and obedience. What is fascinating is that these three terms, often used to show that Anselm was mostly imposing medieval feudalism on the work of redemption, are also three major terms used in the Benedictine Rule. Anselm was a monk first and foremost, and it should not come as a surprise that the monastic vocabulary was the one used by Anselm in his theological works.

If that is the case, we should be careful about supposing that Anselm used secular categories to formulate his theory of the atonement instead of using monastic language that was much more essential to his Christian life. For Anselm the monastic life was the optimal way of living the Christian life, because the monk's life could be entirely dedicated to God, concerned only about the one to whom all things are due. By contrast, lay people have no choice but to live for God *and* for the world (i.e. their family and profession).

The consequence is that order, honour, and obedience are notions that we should understand in Anselm's monastic context. To understand the place and role of "order" in Anselm's theology of the atonement, it will not suffice to merely say that it reflects feudal society's hierarchical order. Anselm's theology of "order" is not about regulating hierarchy. Within the Rule of Benedict, order is essentially accepting a place assigned for one's benefit. "Obedience" refers back to consecration and love. In the Rule of Benedict, obedience is not about following blindly. It is conscious and willing acceptance motivated by the conviction that the "superior" desires and strives for the good of those who owe him obedience. It is not selfish, but a service rendered by the superior to the inferior. It encourages mutual love and respect. Finally, in the Rule "honour" is not a strict hierarchical notion but includes mutual relationships which seal mutual love between the monks. Moreover, honour does not reflect the secular obsession with power and prestige. For the monks, honour is also due to the weakest, and thus is not exclusive. It is due at every level of the monastic hierarchy. This marks the true difference between the Rule's view of "honour" and a secular understanding.

Anselm's most formative social context is certainly the monastic life, and it is there that we should seek the framework necessary to understand him. This conclusion helps us understand our own times. What is the social context, the social order to which we are the most accountable? Where do we have life and being? What gives rule and direction to our lives? These questions are essential because they will help us to be conscious of the manner in which we live out our faith.

Anselm's Theology of the Atonement

Anselm's theology has long been associated, almost exclusively, with his theology of the atonement. Much has been written about it, and its legacy cannot be underestimated. To understand his contribution fully, a grasp of the alternative versions of the atonement is necessary. Anselm interacted, albeit indirectly, with most of them, though in the end he offered his own explanation of the atonement.

One of the most popular theologies of the atonement, at that time, was that of Tertullian. To him, the atonement was essentially a work of satisfaction rendered to God. This was paid through penitential acts and good works, after baptism. These works of justice, obedience, and penitence (including fasting, prayers, and almsgiving), all worked towards the merit of the believer. Repentance was a great work of satisfaction to God. The work of Christ, through His satisfaction of God's law, was a demonstration of God's love for mankind. No human works, however "good", could come close to Christ's fulfilling God's demands. In Tertullian, we find a great emphasis on the meaning of Christ's death as redeeming others. His explanation was, however, open to several criticisms, including that it introduced a doctrine of merits that endangered, or downplayed, the gracious nature of the atonement.

Another common view of the atonement was proposed by Italian monk Rufinus of Aquileia (344/345-411). Satan had gained an unbreakable power over humanity. To redeem His own creatures, God's only option was to deceive Satan. God thus used Christ's humanity as bait to lure Satan into a direct conflict which, because of Christ's divinity, God would win. In God's redeeming plan, Christ's human nature would bait Satan, and His divine nature would make sure that Satan would be hooked until he had no more power over humanity. While Rufinus clearly saw the atonement as God's great victory over Satan, his formulation raised difficult questions about God's omnipotence.

Anselm also rejected the view associated with Irenaeus, according to which the "apostate one", meaning Satan, had taken humanity captive. God's redemptive plan was to ransom mankind by paying the greatest price. Christ sets humanity free from slavery to Satan, manifested in the slavery to sin. With Irenaeus, redemption is mostly interpreted as a ransom paid to Satan, and not to God, and justice as one of God's great motivating attributes.

Classic Christian theology has maintained that God manifested His justice in a twofold manner. First, God manifested His justice in defeating Satan who had unjustly enslaved mankind—made in the image of God. Satan had taken something that did not belong to him, and God restored justice and peace in reconciling mankind with Himself. Second, God acted *justly* according to His attributes, among which were grace and love. For Irenaeus, justice was the essential attribute at play in the process of atonement and was aimed at ransoming mankind from Satan.

While very influential, this explanation gave the impression that God's will was coerced by Satan. God's only choice was to ransom humanity. His choice was determined by Satan's action, thus limiting God's sovereignty. Moreover, the idea that mankind belongs to Satan because of its rebellion against God was not universally accepted. Indeed, there are many problems with that view, including a lack of biblical support.

There were other dimensions of the work of atonement which formed the background to Anselm's own development. One of them was the substitutionary nature of Christ's work. Simply to say that it was substitutionary was not enough. Tertullian and Irenaeus had both clearly discerned that this was an important aspect of Christ's work. The great Augustine also knew as much, but still had difficulty explaining what, precisely, the substitution was for. Of course, Augustine's creative energy was directed at the struggles against heresies: they more or less dictated the direction his theology could take. That he did not have great clarity as to the specific object of Christ's substitutive sacrifice is no real surprise.

In conclusion, the dominant formulations of the atonement, before Anselm, were articulated around the notion of something owed and satisfaction being made. That was the heart of Christ's sacrifice. This does not mean that it was the only thing to say about the atonement. For example, God's victory over Satan was not absent from the theologies of the atonement, but this aspect of redemption tended to be overshadowed by others. The fact that God was victorious was due to the ransoming by God. The means of God's victory was the key to early theologies of the atonement, while the reason for the importance and role of Christ's sacrifice was not clearly apprehended.

Theologians well understood that the fall of humanity made atonement necessary, though difficult questions remained: why did God need a mediator such as Christ? After all, if God was all-powerful and goodness itself, He could well forgive without any satisfaction. If He did need satisfaction, what was it for? In other words, what was the *objective* of Christ's sacrifice? That it was absolutely necessary, there was no doubt. But why was it so?

This is where Anselm offers a great contribution to the theology of the atonement. Anselm's formulation is groundbreaking because he brought clarity and harmony to the nature, process, and objective of the atonement.

First, as to the nature of the atonement, Anselm notes that it is wholly dependent on the entrance of sin into the world. All relationships, including those within mankind as well as between mankind and God, are broken, that is, in need of restoration. Truth, justice, goodness, obedience, and worship: qualities that qualified the relation of communion between God and His creation, have been deeply affected. Mankind is not capable of restoring those, much less re-establishing the cosmic order. Sin was against God and had cosmic proportions; the atonement would have to restore this.

Mankind was unable, because of sin, to render to God truth, justice, goodness, obedience, and worship. Another way to look at the nature of sin, according to Anselm, is to see it as the inability to give God what is owed Him—and through Him, to the whole cosmos. To Anselm, this is only part of the reason. Saying that truth and justice, in particular, are owed to God as creator is not enough. It is owed to Him because He *is* truth and justice. To be in communion with Him required truth and justice. These are not concepts or things owed. They qualify the living relationship between mankind and God.

The cosmic nature of sin should not be underestimated. If God certainly is the affected party in mankind's rebellion, He is not the only one. Humanity's innocent state and blessedness was also affected. If satisfaction were required, it was not only for God, but also for the whole beautiful ordering of the universe, especially for the restoration of mankind's blessedness. Satisfaction should be cosmic in nature and cosmic in scope (Romans 8:18-25).

Second, as for the process of redemption, Anselm is very clear that God willed to effect salvation through the incarnation, not as a fatality but as a means coming both from His loving choice, and also from right and consistent reason. God Himself had to fulfil the demands—satisfy—for truth and justice, and for honour, which included due worship. Jesus lived a life of obedience and love to God, and died on the cross, neither out of blind obedience to justice, nor because it was required of Him against His will by a partial God.

As for sacrifice, it was required because through Adam mankind had rebelled against God the creator, and had not rendered due obedience and worship to God, toward whom they naturally tended, and in whom all qualities were found. All mankind was included in the first head, and because of the original disobedience, mankind lost its inheritance. Mankind could not exercise free will integrally because it was a righteous will that God required. That is exactly what had been lost.

Sacrifice was demanded, not because humanity was required to offer sacrifices, but because God had become man and had to give satisfaction for all that was due to God. The price for mankind was the sacrifice of the God-man. In that sense, God the Father willed that Jesus died not first and foremost for the honour of His name, but to save mankind from its sin. The objection some raise against Anselm, in saying that to the medieval theologian God's honour was the only motivation for salvation, is a gross mischaracterization. Anselm's God is also a gracious and compassionate God.

The atonement had to be a sacrifice, not merely because a despotic God demanded justice, but because goodness and truth also required justice. In His life and death Christ upheld everything that was necessary for humanity itself to be saved. He suffered the death judgement—the infinite sacrifice—demanded for cosmic restoration.

Finally, the objective of the atonement for Anselm was not limited to restoring God's honour. Such a view is often the result of a limited reading of Anselm. We tend to restrict Anselm's theology of the atonement to one book, but his theology is richer and broader than what he writes in *Cur Deus homo?* The ultimate goal of the atonement was cosmic restoration. The Incarnation was not only God descending to mankind assuming our flesh, but also the raising up of humanity in the God-man. Thus, what the atonement accomplished was also the raising up of humanity, its restoration and glorification to the state it had been promised.

For Anselm, Christ's satisfying death was only an element of the objective of redemption. Redemption was a means to an end. It was essential, absolutely necessary, but it was directed at something much larger. What was at stake was not merely a satisfaction for human sin, but the restoration of human nature. True enough, Anselm stressed the reparation for guilt as well as the restoration of God's honour broken by human disobedience. The reparation for those, however, is not the end goal of Christ's work. Anselm would summarise the whole objective of redemption of the restoration of human nature as well as the regaining of blessed immortality. Christ's incarnation serves as the glorification of human nature, the goal God always intended for humanity.

Seeing the atonement in such a light, Anselm established a clearer and stronger biblical relationship between the doctrine of original sin and the goal of redemption. A significant part of the mission of the God-man was to unite Himself with humanity: in the same manner as humanity was united to its first head, Adam. Humanity could now be united to its redeeming head, the second Adam. More than that, the God-man must have something to render to God that is beyond the sin of humanity and, at the same time, must render this not out of obligation, but voluntarily.

Legacy and significance

There is a heated debate about the value of Anselm's formulation of a doctrine of the atonement. One of the most common objections revolves around his decision to use the language of hierarchic feudal society to frame his doctrine of redemption.

In this reading, Anselm interpreted the work of Christ only within the limits of what a feudal system could provide. Hence, the main object of the atonement was to restore God's honour, in the same way that a lord's honour should be restored when blemished by one of his vassals.

Such a stress on preserving, defending or restoring God's honour might paint Him as a petty and jealous God concerned more about His own name than His creation. The only thing that would move God to become man is not love for humanity, but a desire to see His honour restored. Compassion for sinners would not be a true motivation for the atonement. It is concluded that this is not the God of the Scriptures. It would be a god made in the image of Anselm's society, with all the limitations of that society. If that was really Anselm's theology of the atonement, the critics would be right: Anselm's theory would be extremely limited.

We should pause for a moment however. When we read Anselm putting so much emphasis on the honour of God, and knowing he is a theologian of the eleventh-century, we logically assume that he is a dependent, or even a prisoner, of his social context. That is an interesting point because it demands we first go back to Anselm's time and define "honour" accordingly.

We should note three things about Anselm's definition of "honour". To begin with, Anselm's contextual use of "honour" includes the analogy of a servant having tarnished his master's owner, debt that could be only cancelled by the guilty party or by someone belonging to the master's very own family. This conditioned, in great part, Anselm's view of the necessity of satisfaction. Further, Anselm takes great care to present God's honour as a double reality: service and worship. In his medieval context, God's honour is not only judicial and procedural. Honour leads to worship. That is why, finally, the notion of honour included the whole cosmos. All of creation, both animate and inanimate, man and beast, and the rest of the natural world, was in a state of harmonious order. Everything was created and preserved in its good and due place. Defined in this way, God's honour expresses the beauty and order of the universe which is directed to God as its originator and creator.

This had a profound impact on the theology of sin and the atonement. As God's representatives, the first humans' sin was the disfiguration of the just and good ordering of the world. Thus, atonement did not concern first the personal honour of God. It included the integrity of the whole cosmos. Fascinatingly, this means that when the first human sin compromised God's honour, it also compromised humanity's integrity, its relationship to the natural world, and to God.

Anselm certainly did use the language of his day. That he was influenced by his own society is also quite probable. After all, there is no theology that is so uprooted from its social context as to be free from all social influence. To be understood, we always use words and concepts familiar to our contemporaries. The problem is not that we use such and such language, but whether we are bound to it. Anselm was not, and was able to integrate in his definition of God's honour, a set of theological convictions that went beyond a mere feudal definition of honour.

Conclusion

While there has been strong criticism directed at Anselm for presenting an overly legal and judicial view of the atonement, we should refrain from limiting Anselm to a predetermined set of affirmations. That is the problem with common objections: they too often eclipse the actual nature of what is being criticised. Thus, in the case of Anselm, we should be cautious before interpreting his theology of the atonement purely as one of legal satisfaction. Anselm's focus, however, is not exclusively on reparation for guilt. This is not the goal, merely an instrument towards a goal which is the restoration of humanity.

Anselm's theology of the atonement reminds us of the wonderful grace and sacrifice offered in order to secure our redemption. "Why did God become man?" is a question we must take seriously because it recapitulates considerations about who God is, the nature of man, our relationship with our loving creator, the nature of sin, and the scope of redemption. Today, there is a renewed opposition to the theology of substitution. To many in the Evangelical world, such a theology of the atonement is unacceptable. The God of substitutionary atonement is portrayed as God the Father abusing His Son, or as the action of a bloodthirsty God who cannot save but through sacrifice.

Anselm's insights would mark the subsequent theologies of the atonement until the 18th and 19th centuries. His stress on the cosmic goal of the atonement is still relevant today. What Anselm had in view, was a complete restoration of the universal created order. In an age of global ethics, of creation care, and renewed focus on community life, Anselm's theology of the atonement is a great example of a theology so focused on God that it includes all of creation.

Bernard of Clairvaux
(1090-1153)

Love of Christ and of the Word

Biographical sketch

This sketch cannot provide the full context for the world into which Bernard was born but it does lay down some of the more important markers. He was born in 1090 to a father and mother who certainly appear devout by the standards of their time. His father not only ultimately answered the call to go on the First Crusade but later died while far from home. Though Bernard was a dutiful son it would appear that, just as Monica had a strong influence on Augustine, so Bernard was most strongly influenced by his mother. Her dying wish was that Bernard, her oldest son, would enter the monastery. Seven years later he overcame the reluctance of his father by reminding him of that wish. His father, as a member of the martial part of feudal society, inevitably wanted Bernard to follow in his footsteps. It is a testimony to Bernard that in his early 20s he convinced others to seek the monastic life with him: he entered with some thirty others, amongst whom were a couple of his uncles and some of his brothers. Ultimately all of his five brothers and even his father would take holy orders, joining the Cistercians.

As a further sign of his prominence amongst his peers he was sent as founding abbot to the Valley of Wormwood. By his leadership and industry, he and his fellow monks transformed it into the Clear Valley or, in French, Clairvaux. For four decades Clairvaux would be the place to which he would always return no matter how far afield his labours would take him. By the time of his death, Clairvaux was the mother or grandmother of almost 170 houses and the Cistercian community, which had grown to over 10,000 strong. By any standards Bernard of Clairvaux was a most remarkable man.

Historical context

When dealing with any historical figure it is necessary to take a moment to understand the era in which they were raised—indeed, the further removed from our own day, the greater the need. However it does raise the difficult question of just how far back one has to go. When the days of Bernard of Clairvaux are as distant to our own the problem is compounded. What from use and want now seems to us so obvious as to require no explanation would be inexplicable to the high medieval mind. Equally, that which would seem commonplace to those of the twelfth century is in danger not only of appearing wrong, but a huge moral blight to us today.

In evaluating the life of Bernard of Clairvaux, the context becomes not so much a helpful background but essential to our understanding. Events from centuries before still made their effects known and, if not entirely exonerating, then at least make understandable the choice made by one who is arguably the most significant figure of the twelfth century.

In the fourth century, Emperor Constantine had moved his capital from Rome to Byzantium, renaming it Constantinople. The absence of any imperial presence in the ancient capital of the Roman Empire inevitably enhanced not only the prestige of the pope, but his political importance. As imperial power waned in the West, those of the Germanic tribes, ever ready for an opportunity to plunder, crossed the boundaries and assisted in the dismantling of the structures of society to which the Empire had given rise. As the cities became the focus of pillaging, those who desired to maintain their Christian faith sought refuge in separated communities. Initially begun with rules for communal living, life in the monastery included a strict regime of labour and devotions. With the passing of time, they accrued considerable wealth. The reasons are not hard to find. With the passage of centuries, notable monasteries had been bequeathed tracts of land (the most significant identifier of wealth in a feudal society) as well as some of the more obvious statements of significant financial resources.

Though, in charity, we might allow that the generous benefactors acted out of piety, one consequence was that the increased wealth of a monastery meant that the monks themselves were no longer required to fulfil the same rigorous approach to daily life. For those who longed for the stricter codes of an earlier stage, many of the opportunities for the contemplative life seemed to be lacking. The Benedictine Order was one that appeared to have fallen victim to its own success. It is perhaps something of an indication of the future hopes and desires of Bernard that rather than pursuing the monastic life within a Benedictine monastery he chose, at around the age of twenty-two, to enter the Cistercian Order. Though finding their origins in the Benedictine Order, the Cistercians sought to return to a style of monasticism that was more rigorous. Indeed Bernard himself, in his strict habit of rising long before dawn and consistently depriving himself of sleep, did damage to his own health. In later life he required a place set aside near to the place of devotions so that he would be able to withdraw in order to vomit.

A further consequence of the emperor's removal from Rome and the increase in prestige of the pope was the Great Schism of 1054, less than forty years before the birth of Bernard. In that fateful year the pope in Rome and the Patriarch of Constantinople excommunicated one another—a division which remains with us to this day. The pope's claim to ultimate authority was, at least in his own eyes, unanswerable: he was Bishop of the See where both Peter and Paul were martyred. With the rise of Islam, the successors of Mohammed swept through the Middle East, Egypt, along the North African littoral and up into Spain. Their advance was finally halted at the battle of Tours in 732 by the grandfather of Charlemagne, Charles Martel. Aside from the geopolitical impact of the advance of Islam, the former significant centres of Christianity, with only the exceptions of Rome and Constantinople, were now in the hands of Muslims. That made the contest for the role of *primus inter pares* (first among equals), if not outright ultimate authority, a debate between two cities, only one of which had any historical claim to having been significant in the life of the Church from the beginning.

The decline and reformation of the monastic orders, the rise of the Papacy, the division of Christendom and the rise of Islam were all factors that would have an impact on Bernard.

Legacy

This slim volume is not merely a compendium of some of the most remarkable men from 500 to 1500 but is written with the desire to give confidence that during those thousand years the light of the Gospel had not been entirely extinguished. Through providing some of the background and context we desire to explain some of the issues that may give rise to concern. This can help us to appreciate the issues encountered, and not see them only in a negative light.

Where a Protestant would have difficulty in keeping company with Bernard is in his devotion to Mary. Observing even just some of its worst excesses in the Roman Catholic Church has produced in many a Protestant such an aversion that they will hardly mention her name for fear of taking a step in that direction. It is true that Bernard speaks of Mary in such a way that would cause most, if not all, thinking Protestants to shrink back, but at least we can take comfort in the knowledge that he resisted some of the worst elements of Mariolatry. In 1140 when the Canons of Lyons proposed a festival in honour of the Immaculate Conception he came out in opposition. The grounds for his opposition are encouraging inasmuch as he argued that it was contrary to Scripture. Though there were other elements that perhaps we hold as being no less contrary to Scripture, when pressed too far, he was willing to take a stand.

Bernard has also been criticised for his stance against Abelard and for the vehemence of his opposition, as well as the way he used his influence effectively to silence one recognised to be a significant intellect of his age. At the heart of the debate lay a difference in approach. For Bernard faith came first and reason was to be applied in its support. For Abelard reason came first and faith was to be reviewed in its light. Inevitably such a gross oversimplification will have its weaknesses, but the debate between Bernard and Abelard was something of a foreshadowing of the debates between those who would fall for the rationalism of the Enlightenment, and those who would nevertheless maintain a commitment to the authority and inspiration of Scripture. Perhaps there is nothing new under the sun after all. The detractors of Bernard accused him of using his standing against Abelard and his supporters, and that his opponent was never able to present his opinions and argue his case himself. Again, Bernard had effectively acted as "king-maker" when a dispute arose over who was the rightful pope. The next pope was a former student of Bernard, and he was able to ensure that Abelard was taken under protection only to die a year later. This meant that Abelard was not able to propagate his opinions as widely as he desired.

But perhaps the greatest concern arises out of his preaching of the Second Crusade. For many that may be enough to damn him without further explanation. Not only does that show a failure to judge a man in the context of the age in which he lives but may show a lack of understanding of the causes of the Crusades themselves.

Initially, Islam had advanced by the power of the sword, and seemed unstoppable for the first hundred years after the death of Mohammed in 632. That is, until it was stopped at the Battle of Tours in 732. After that the Muslim East and the Christian

West had settled down into a period of more or less peaceful coexistence. In the broadest terms, from around A.D. 800 to 1000, Christians in the West had been going on pilgrimage to the Holy Sites and a veritable tourist industry had grown up that welcomed the Christians, provided hospitality, and marketed the sort of trinkets that are still available to this day in street bazaars. So what changed? Those who would be described as "moderate Muslims" holding sway over the Muslim world were challenged by the Seljuk Turks—they were the Islamists of their day. These were fiercely aggressive Muslims who first occupied the eastern part of what is modern-day Turkey and continued to move westward until they were across the narrow strip of water that separates Asia from Europe at Constantinople. The Emperor could literally see from his palace window the camp of those who had invaded his territory and appropriated it for themselves. Of course, they had done nothing different to what many another conquering army had done, and done so in the time-honoured method of force of arms.

The response of the Emperor was just as clear and that was to seek to drive back those who had invaded his lands, if not by force of his own arms, then by enlisting others to come to his aid. Thus it was that the Emperor sought assistance from the pope in Rome. The aggression that precipitated the First Crusade was not Western expansionism or sheer bloodlust on the part of an under-utilised military cast, but in response to a plea from separated brethren in the East. When this was combined with the stories of those who had managed to get back from a pilgrimage to the Holy Sites of being robbed and of massacres of bands of pilgrims, the stage was set for an armed response. It has to be said that the objectives of Emperor and pope had little in common. The Emperor was making a plea for military assistance to reclaim land he had lost to the Seljuk Turks. The pope, no doubt with an eye to enhancing his own prestige as a significant political player in the West, and pressing his claim to having ultimate ecclesiastical authority, encouraged the launch of the First Crusade. It ended with the capture of Jerusalem, noted for the slaughter of its inhabitants. Though one cannot excuse the wholesale massacre of men, women, and children, this too needs to be considered in its own context. When a besieging army surrounds a city, the rulers of the city have basically two options. They can surrender and throw themselves on the mercy of the invading force. Other cities had done precisely that on the Crusaders' march towards Jerusalem and received favourable terms of surrender. The alternative was to compel the invaders to take it by force, making it as costly as possible for them in the hope that either sickness, disease, and lack of supplies would weaken their resolve or a relief army would arrive to drive them away. If they took the latter option the citizens could expect no mercy. That would be the price that they would have to pay for resisting. If there were no penalty for a city that resisted, then all would do it. Harsh it undoubtedly was, but not without a certain logic, on purely military terms.

Similarly, when the Crusader city of Edessa fell in 1144, all those who were not able to flee to the citadel for refuge were slaughtered. This was the event that precipitated the Second Crusade. We may indeed find the nature of medieval warfare distressing and for good reason, but viewing it in its context, while not providing an excuse, will at least lend us some understanding.

Bernard's own father, then, had gone off to the First Crusade in response to the aggression of the Seljuk Turks and the plea from the Emperor and had died seeking to secure the path of pilgrimage and the Holy Sites. The Crusaders had retaken territory by force and the forces of Islam had responded in like fashion. Much blood had been shed on both sides. Perhaps we might have wished Bernard to remain silent, but it is perhaps understandable that in the context of his day he perceived a militant Islam to be a threat to Christendom and hastened to its defence. There are indications that when he became aware that not all that was done in the name of Christ was in the least Christian, that he came to regret the role that he had played.

Theological relevance

If not all that might be said about Bernard of Clairvaux can be unequivocally entered on the positive side of the ledger then there are at least some that can be. In the monastic rule which he followed, all the Psalms were recited every week. The Bible itself was read from first to last on a regular basis and Bernard himself was noted as one who continually read through Scripture from start to finish. If a man entered the monastery illiterate, he would learn to read by studying the text of the Bible. What marked Bernard out in particular was his close adherence to the text of God's word. Reading through his sermons and other written works one cannot help but note the frequency with which he cites Scripture, sometimes with as much as fifteen or more references in one page. It is his commitment to the authority of Scripture that perhaps, more than anything else, earned him the gratitude of both Luther and Calvin. The former held him to be one of the greatest doctors of the Church. The latter referred to him more than any other medieval theologian. And though he was not above disagreeing with Bernard, Calvin very often commended him most warmly, thinking him the major witness to the truth between Gregory the Great who died in 604 and the dawn of the Reformation.

Calvin recognised that Bernard followed in the theology of Augustine and held clearly that sinners depend on God, and on God alone, for their salvation. In Bernard's theology no one can be converted to the Lord unless the Lord wills it first and calls him with an inner voice. The conversion of sinners is clearly the work of divine grace.

But let Bernard speak for himself:

Which of us, if he suddenly noticed that the clothing which covers him was spattered all over with filth and the foulest mud, would not be violently disgusted and quickly take it off and cast it from him indignantly?

When I reflect, as I often do, on the ardor with which the patriarchs long for the incarnation of Christ, I am pierced with sorrow and shame.

And now I can scarcely contain my tears, so ashamed am I of the lukewarmness and lethargy of the present times. For which of us is filled with joy at the realisation of this grace as the holy men of old were moved to desire by the promise of it?

I am with that Sinner, that outlaw, that wicked man. I am a Sinner because I have sinned, an outlaw because I deliberately and persistently go against the law.

Whatever else might be said of Bernard, he loved Christ. This comes through again and again both in his sermons and in his other written works, but perhaps nowhere more clearly than in his hymns which still rejoice the hearts of saints to this day:

> "O sacred head now wounded
> With grief and shame weighed down,
> Now scornfully surrounded
> With thorns thine only crown.
>
> How art thou pale with anguish,
> With sore abuse and scorn!
> How does that visage languish,
> Which once was bright as morn!
>
> What language shall I borrow
> To thank thee dearest friend?
> For this, thy dying sorrow,
> Thy pity without end.
>
> O make me thine forever,
> And should I fainting be,
> Lord, let me never, ever
> Outlive my love to thee."

And again:

> "Jesus, the very thought of thee
> with sweetness fills my breast;
> but sweeter far thy face to see,
> and in thy presence rest.
>
> O hope of every contrite heart,
> O joy of all the meek,
> to those who fall, how kind thou art!
> How good to those who seek!
>
> But what to those who find? Ah, this
> nor tongue nor pen can show;
> the love of Jesus, what it is,
> none but his loved ones know.
>
> Jesus, our only joy be thou,
> as thou our prize wilt be;
> Jesus, be thou our glory now,
> and through eternity."

Conclusion

A study of the life of Bernard of Clairvaux demonstrates the difficulty of understanding the life and circumstances of someone who lived centuries ago. In Bernard's case we are only a little short of a millennium ago! Even when we do our best to make allowances for the context of a life so very different to our own, we still must recognise that we do not fully comprehend the impact of the passing of the years. We would all like to think that had we lived in an era when slavery was considered acceptable, and even defended, by Christian scholars that somehow we would have stood firmly and resolutely in opposition. If we had been born into Nazi Germany though great swathes of the population may have been duped by the evil, we would have resisted even at the cost of our lives. Perhaps. It is more likely, however, that we would have accepted as all but unquestionable the prevailing culture and failed either to raise a concern or pry into matters that might prove injurious to our health.

It is too easy to accept the understanding of the Scriptures which we received from parent or pastor and assume that all who have gone before us would have seen everything we see with the same clarity.

There are indeed matters of theology and interpretation accepted by Bernard with which we would have to take issue. Was his theology flawless? We would have to say that it was not. That in itself should actually lend us a degree of humility as we would ask ourselves the question as to what we may have accepted for less than adequate reasons, and, if the Lord should tarry, which future generation will wonder why we did not see what is so obvious to them.

What we can still affirm, with all these caveats, is that Bernard had a high view of Scripture and that he sought to test all opinions against its teachings. He did so according to the light that he had. Beyond that we can surely say that his love of God's word fuelled his love of Christ. He was convinced that it was only through Christ that a man can be right with God and that was the message he preached.

Peter Waldo (1140–1205)
Scriptures: The Highest Authority

Biographical sketch

From Bernard and the Abbey at Clairvaux we make our way almost exactly south to Lyon: nearly 200 miles and 100 years later to encounter Peter Waldo. These two men could hardly be more different in many ways, but in the matters which count they were very much the same. Bernard of Clairvaux was arguably the best-known name of his generation—even his century. He was already an abbot in his twenties and remained in ecclesiastical office until his death four decades later. He was officially recognised as a doctor of the Church and nicknamed "Doctor Mellifluous"—the honey-tongued preacher. He was the confidant and advisor to popes and directly involved in the most significant political event of his day.

Contrast this with Peter Waldo. There is more than one rendering of his last name and his first name may be more of a nickname than his actual given name. He was not an ordained man in any sense and held no office in the Church. The ecclesiastical authorities wanted to silence him and did not promote his teachings. His followers faced fierce persecution to the point of death. And yet, by the grace of God, they survived down to the Reformation and even to this day in the very lands where once they were hunted and oppressed. Indeed, those who would style themselves Waldensians can, with some accuracy, declare that theirs was the first Reformation more than 300 years before Luther and Calvin, and that they held the flame of the Gospel aloft for centuries before the magisterial reformers first drew breath.

Neither Waldo nor his successors aspired to the academy and such written works as they might have bequeathed were oft-times seized and destroyed with them so as to leave little written trace except in the annals of their persecutors. For that reason, certainty eludes the historian, and much is left to conjecture. Waldo was not trained in theology or canon law but was a merchant, probably dealing in cloth. As a young man there appear to have been two significant episodes which were, in a very real sense, life-changing. Not even the sequence is clear but perhaps that does not matter as each seems to have confirmed the other. At some merchant gathering a young man, only a little older than himself, suddenly died. Whether he choked to death on something he was eating or whether he abruptly dropped dead from a heart attack is unclear. What is clear is the impact it had on Waldo. He was deeply sensible of the fragility of life and convicted that it could have been his own life that had been so abruptly cut short.

A second incident around the same time also played into the thinking of the young Waldo. It may have been a wandering minstrel or some other itinerant entertainer who gave voice to a religious song about the rich young ruler of the Gospels. The rich young ruler came with a question to Jesus as to what he must do to inherit eternal life. To this Jesus replied that he should sell all that he had, give to the poor and come follow Him.

Whichever of these two incidents came first, the response of Waldo was to seek greater clarity from the Word of God. Such a desire would seem natural to us and easily answered. Not so when Waldo was wrestling with matters of eternal life. The Scriptures were not available in the common tongue of the people and Waldo's knowledge of Latin was limited. What he did have were the resources to pay scholars to translate the Scriptures from Latin into French-Provençal. (French as it is read today was not an option.) This emphasis on the Scripture alone predated the watchword of the Reformation, *Sola Scriptura*, by hundreds of years. Waldo and his followers emphasised the necessity of knowing and applying the word of God. Though he lived a hundred years after Bernard and there was much to distinguish between them, in this they were very much alike. Generations later, and yet before the invention of the printing press, the emphasis on knowing and applying the word of God still marked the Waldensians apart. In the communities in which they worshipped, individual families would be assigned different books of the Bible to commit to memory.

As Waldo read Scripture he saw that there were significant differences between what he had been raised to believe and what he was reading. The story of the rich young ruler seemed to have personal application to him and so he resolved to follow the words of Christ to the rich young ruler and live a life of poverty. As he was married with two daughters, he made over to them his property so that they would be taken care of but gave the rest of his wealth away. He then begged for his daily bread. Inevitably, such a course of action from one who was once a rich merchant now begging on the streets of Lyon brought him to the attention of the authorities. On one level the solution was simple: he was permitted to beg but only from his wife and not from the general population. But his begging was not the only concern— especially of the Archbishop of Lyon. He was also preaching the message that he was reading in translated Scriptures. He was warned to keep silence because he, as a member of the laity, had no authority to preach. His response was that of Peter before the Sanhedrin who, in a similar position, declared that he had to obey God, not man. This may be the origin of his being called "Peter" not because that was actually his name, but because at that crucial meeting, he said what the apostle said. The first occurrence of Waldo being called Peter is more than a hundred years after his death.

An emphasis on Scripture

The trajectory of the life and witness of Peter Waldo becomes obvious. Confronted with his own mortality, he came under conviction from the Word of God. Though we do not have access to the Lamb's Book of Life, it seems reasonable to suppose that he passed through a conversion experience which led him to divest himself of his worldly wealth as a merchant after making provision for his wife and daughters. Waldo was not content to merely make a personal statement of piety however, but began to declare publicly his faith in Christ and urge others to follow. Others did, too, which inevitably brought him to the attention of the authorities.

Unfortunately, Peter Waldo's general approach was contrary to that of the church at that time. It wasn't that vows of poverty were against the ethos of the day. Quite the opposite. Bernard of Clairvaux was a strong advocate of a rigorous regime for the Cistercians. Francis of Assisi, who was broadly a contemporary of Waldo, and perhaps the best-known of the medieval saints, was likewise a strong advocate for renouncing the comforts of the world. The problem was not embracing poverty. If anything, there were too many such groupings springing up and many of them desired official recognition. That was not the issue. The real concern was that Waldo was engaging in open-air preaching and that was a challenge to the office of the priesthood. Only those who were ordained to the priesthood had the officially recognised authority to expound God's word. By preaching in public he was challenging the Church's monopoly on the right to interpret Scripture. As those Scriptures were in Latin, maintaining the monopoly in the context of a society that no longer spoke Latin was much easier. Having those Scriptures translated into the vernacular was, though perhaps unintentional on Waldo's part, a challenge in and of itself.

As for Bernard, and indeed for all those who have lived in a different age far removed from our own, it becomes necessary to ask what the trends in society were against which the life of any individual should be measured. Within a few years of the death of Waldo, pope Innocent III called the Fourth Lateran Council. In 1215, the same year that the barons in England were curbing the authority of the king by compelling him to sign the Magna Carta, Innocent III was seeking to consolidate the authority of the Church. It was at the Council that marriage was brought within the sphere of ecclesiastical regulation. As a result the Church determined who was and who was not legally married, and not just that, but whether the offspring of any particular union was deemed to be legitimate or not. Establishing legal succession was of significant value to society but it was also very clearly advantageous in establishing the power of the Church.

At the same time the doctrine of transubstantiation was being developed in ecclesiastical circles. The significance with regard to Waldo was that this, too, promoted the authority of the priesthood. It was by virtue of the Apostolic succession transmitted through the pope that the local ordained clergy could, according to this theology, transform the elements of communion into the body and blood of Christ. Again, the authority of the priesthood was being underlined at a time when Waldo, in his understanding of what it meant to be a Christian, was going about the streets telling others of faith in Christ. In hindsight one can see the trend. Only priests had the authority to preach and declare what Scriptures taught. Only priests could marry and declare who was legitimate offspring or not. Only priests could turn the elements of communion into the body and blood of Christ and without communion eternal salvation itself was put in doubt.

It does not appear that Waldo was setting out to challenge the power and authority of the priesthood, but it was an inevitable consequence of his actions. For his part, he sought to be in humble submission to the Church and did not seem to be seeking to cast himself in the role of challenging the established rule. On the contrary, Waldo's response was to desire to lay his opinions before the pope for a definitive declaration. This he did but was sent away without an answer. It would appear that those hearing his arguments concluded that he was doing much the same as Paul, as recorded in the Acts of the Apostles and in the epistles, and with much the same effect. One might have hoped that that would have led them to support Waldo in his every endeavour. On the contrary, they concluded after his departure that he had to desist from his activities.

At the Synod of Verona in 1184 Waldo and his followers were excommunicated. Worse was to come in the Fourth Lateran Council in which Innocent III formally declared Waldo and his followers heretics, in spite of their previous perceptions.

Waldo continued to declare Christ and others joined him. His background was not in ecclesiastical office, and he had received no formal theological training. His background was as a merchant, and it can be seen in the way he set about presenting the gospel and in the way in which his followers likewise sought to make Christ known. As a merchant he would present his wares and as the transaction was nearing its conclusion declare to his client that he had a pearl of unequalled price which he wished to show him or her. The pearl was, of course, the Gospel. At other times verses from Scripture would be copied out and left among the goods being sold. Long before Gospel tracts were being printed and placed in the hands of passers-by on busy streets, 800 years ago Waldo and his followers were distributing their own handwritten tracts.

It does not appear that Waldo ever set out deliberately to challenge the authority of the Church. Hundreds of years later, Luther declared, "My conscience is captive to the Word of God. Thus, I cannot and will not recant, because acting against one's conscience is neither safe nor sound. Here I stand; I can do no other. God help me." Waldo was saying much the same.

From Waldo to Luther

For those of us brought up in a world with a bewildering array of denominations and many churches that declare they are non-denominational, the idea of ministry outside of "organised religion" is more than possible and might even be preferable. At the time of the Reformation the fracturing of the Church into a multiplicity of independent bodies became a reality, though even in separating from the Church of Rome, Protestant churches often desired to maintain that there was still only one church even if that church was not the Church of Rome. Thus, for example, when the Reformation came to Scotland in 1560 the Church was simply the Church of Scotland and really remained a single entity until arguably 1711 when the Episcopal Church of Scotland arose.

For Waldo, separating from "the Church" was not his avowed desire though challenging some of its doctrines most certainly was. It is to those doctrines that we now turn in demonstration of the overall thesis of this work—that the light of Biblical truth, and particularly the Gospel, was not entirely extinguished.

Four hundred years before Luther was nailing his 95 Theses to the church door at Wittenberg, the Waldensians had already drawn up their own statement of faith. It was a brief statement, only fourteen paragraphs long, but is unlikely to raise any concerns for the vast majority of members in evangelical churches today. They were at pains to declare their orthodoxy so they began with a clear statement of their adherence to the ancient credal statement known as the Apostles' Creed. They continued by declaring their Trinitarian credentials. They recognised the Scriptures as being the Word of God, telling us of God's creation and the fall of man. As they dealt with the need for salvation their theology emphasised the uniqueness of the Son's work of redemption. According to the Waldensians, the Father sent the Son: "Christ had been promised to the fathers who received the law, to the end that, knowing their sin by the law, and their unrighteousness and insufficiency, they might desire the coming of Christ to make satisfaction for their sins, and to accomplish the law by Himself." "Christ was born [at] a time when iniquity everywhere abounded, to make it manifest that it was not for the sake of any good in ourselves, for all were sinners, but that He, who is true, might display His grace and mercy towards us." "Christ is our life, and truth, and peace, and righteousness - our shepherd and advocate, our sacrifice and priest, who died for the salvation of all who should believe, and rose again for their justification." They went on to declare "that there is no other mediator, or advocate with God the Father, but Jesus Christ". Though they held the Virgin Mary in high honour they rejected any notion of her having any part to play in the salvation of men. They denied the existence of purgatory while affirming the existence of heaven and hell. They went on to abhor the inventions of men in religion such as the observance of special days, abstaining from meat on certain days and going still further in their allusions to penance and pilgrimages as having their origins in the Antichrist.

As the Church of Rome was moving in the direction of specifying seven sacraments, the Waldensians were firm in their conviction that there were only two: baptism and the Lord's Supper and though their use was proper and necessary, nevertheless they maintained that believers may be saved without these signs, when they have neither place nor opportunity of observing them.

Conclusion

Peter Waldo was neither a churchman nor trained theologian but came to firm convictions nevertheless. He saw the fragility of life and gave himself to making known the Gospel to those who would listen to him, gathering a band of followers who in turn declared the Gospel. It was the Scriptures that had led to his conversion, and he was concerned that the Word of God should be made known to others in its beauty and simplicity using his own resources to have Scripture translated from the Latin Vulgate Bible into the common tongue. That translation was among the first translations to be put into the hands of ordinary people. The Word of God was held in high honour by Waldensians who committed entire books to memory and sought to place even short phrases into the hands of those who were open to the Gospel message. They held that Christ alone brought salvation and that believers were justified by faith in Him and that salvation was limited to those who placed their trust in Christ. Their statement of faith was not developed in detail but there was nothing in it that Calvin could not also have affirmed though he came almost four hundred years later.

Bonaventure (1221–1274)

Instructed by God's wisdom

Biographical sketch

Giovanni di Fidanza, Bonaventure's given name, was born in the small medieval town of Bagnorea, about ninety miles from Rome, in 1221. His parents were not of a noble family but had enough means to encourage the education of their children, one of Bonaventure's brothers becoming Canon of the cathedral of Bagnorea. We do not know much about his childhood, nor about how he came to bear the name Bonaventure.

It is quite possible in his birthplace, being close to Assisi, that he came to hear the preachers of the Franciscan order. They were very active in these parts of Italy and their influence was growing rapidly. We know that he entered the Franciscan community between 1238 and 1243, and later studied at the University of Paris under Alexander of Hales, the first Franciscan to hold a chair of theology there. In 1248, Bonaventure became "biblical bachelor" which gave him the right to teach publicly.

The quiet life of a Franciscan brother was not what providence held for Bonaventure. The year 1257 was important for him. After years of opposition between the university and several mendicant orders, among which were the Dominicans and Franciscans, the University of Paris authorised these students to receive their degrees. Bonaventure, along with Thomas Aquinas, received the title of Doctor on 23 October 1257. He was then allowed to teach as one of the professors of the university.

The most important event of 1257, though, was his election as Minister General of the Friars Minor on 2 February 1257. He was then only thirty-six years old. This nomination came with great responsibility. The Order was suffering from a lack of internal unity and organisation, following Francis of Assisi's refusal to govern the Franciscans and his retreat to the sanctuary of La Verna.

Bonaventure spent the next three years providing the Order with a renewed sense of unity and purpose. He achieved this through three policies. Firstly, Bonaventure tried to heal the division between the "Spirituals", who desired to apply the original rule of Francis rigidly, and the "Conventuals", who allowed for certain flexibility with the monastic rule. Secondly, Bonaventure bridged this divide through the promulgation of revised constitutions, and the elimination of the great diversity of preferences and opinions spreading throughout the different branches of the Franciscans. Thirdly, he tried to consolidate monastic unity by producing the official biography of Francis of Assisi, at the request of the Franciscans. This life of Francis was presented in 1263, and officially approved. This united the Franciscans around the figure of their canonised founder.

Under his leadership, other orders joined the Franciscans. For example, in 1264, Bonaventure accepted the request sent by Cardinal Cajetan to take over the direction of the Poor Clares, an order that had been founded in 1212. He did this not out of a desire to control, but to serve. He thus required that the Clares declare, on occasion, that their relationship with the Friars was not one of obligation, but one of charity. This integration into the Franciscans is one of the high points of Bonaventure's leadership. These efforts rightly make Bonaventure the secondary founder of the Franciscans. For the next seventeen years he directed the Franciscans, trying to infuse greater spiritual energy into monastic life.

In 1266 Bonaventure convoked a meeting to further standardise the Friars' relationship to the figure of Francis. In 1269, Bonaventure convened another meeting during which it was decided that a Mass in honour of the Virgin Mary be offered every Sunday. That, of course, raises concerns for Protestant sensibilities. It should be noted, however, that the Mass did not include mention of Mary's immaculate conception. Neither Bonaventure, nor his great contemporary Thomas Aquinas, defended this view, according to which Mary was free from the stain of original sin. It was another Franciscan, Duns Scotus, who set the stage for what would become the official Roman Catholic dogma of the Immaculate Conception. It was only in 1854 that Pius IX declared this doctrine to be an official dogma when he issued the papal bull, *Ineffabilis Deus*.

Through his leadership of the Franciscan order, Bonaventure displayed great Christian virtues, especially charity and wisdom. It is no surprise, then, that his advice on theological and ecclesiastical matters was greatly valued. When time came to elect a new pope, he suggested the name of Theobald Visconti of Piacenza, who was duly elected pope on 1st September 1271, taking the name of Gregory X. Had he known that the new pope would make him a cardinal in 1273, maybe Bonaventure would have revised his choice!

In 1274, Bonaventure retired from the government of the Order when Jerome of Ascoli, who would later be elected pope as Nicholas V, was chosen to replace him. That did not mean that Bonaventure was free from a life of cares. His theological acuity, as well as his personal relationship to the pope, led Gregory X to ask Bonaventure to prepare the theological questions concerned with the reconciliation of Western and Eastern Churches. This was one of the most important topics to be addressed by the Fourteenth Council of Lyon, held in 1274. The aim was none other than mending the Great Schism that had divided Christendom in 1054.

That was no small task, for the divide was by then profound. The crusaders' sack of Constantinople in 1204, during the Fourth Crusade, had remained a major obstacle to the reconciliation between East and West. This was heightened by the temporal rulers in both the East and the West. They repeatedly sought to control the Church and politics, resulting in ecclesiastical conflicts involving both. Moreover, Eastern and Western churches disagreed on an important point of trinitarian theology, called the *Filioque* clause, which was inserted into the Apostles' Creed by the Western Church. The issue was that Churches in the West confessed that God's Spirit proceeded from the Father *and the Son*, in contrast to the Eastern Church whose confession omitted those words. Much was made of this difference and accusations of heresy had been made by both sides. Things were more complicated: by the thirteenth century, East and West had evolved in language and culture, which made theological consensus difficult to reach. In his papal mission, Bonaventure had to take this complex history into account. After much discussion, theologians of the Latin and Greek churches accepted the union on 6 July 1274, though for political reasons this union was never actually implemented. This was Bonaventure's last major act, as he died on Sunday 15 July 1274.

Context: the crisis of the Mendicant orders and Aristotelianism

Bonaventure's life and ministry were deeply marked by the controversy opposing the Mendicant orders and the theological authorities of the universities, in particular that of Paris. The Mendicants, as the name suggests, placed a great emphasis on the vow of poverty, which to them was essential to a true spiritual life. It had been the life of our Lord, and it should also be the path of those committed to following in his footsteps. This could only lead them to a direct confrontation with a Church that had to exercise more caution, and be more flexible with the rich and the nobility of the world.

The issue, though, was not only the question of poverty. The Mendicants proved to be a great social and ecclesiastical force, one that had a significant impact on their society through their consecration and example. The problem was that, in this role, they infringed on the place and role of the

Church, ordinarily centred around parish life. Their loyalty to the pope, who granted them great privileges, one of which was relative independence from episcopal authority, became a major problem. They claimed to have a special role as confessors, and by consequence, to be able to dispense God's forgiveness. This, coupled with great preaching and expository skills made their movements a real social threat to many clerics and nobles in society.

The charisma of the Mendicants threatened the efforts of the parishes, where Church reform was always trying to take root. It is quite ironic that their radicalism could endanger the possibility of reform. They took the moral and theological high ground, not thinking that they might weaken the Church. This should be a warning to us. When striving to implement a new vision for the Church, we should be aware that in so doing, we might also be endangering the rest of the Church. This calls not for inaction, but for prudence and wisdom. In every endeavour, we should be conscious that we belong to a mystical Body that goes beyond our own limited vision for the universal Body of Christ.

The controversy about the Mendicants erupted in 1256, when the former regent of the University of Paris published a treatise against them. This led Bonaventure to publish his great *Defence of the Mendicants*. In this major work, Bonaventure defended the spiritual life, as set by the example of Francis of Assisi. Whether his work helped bridge the divide with the university is unclear. The doctors of the Mendicant orders argued theologically and biblically for the implications of the vow of poverty. The problem was that for their opponents, there were other realities, both social and economic, to which someone like Bonaventure never gave any answer.

The controversy only ended in 1255 when pope Alexander IV annulled the decision of the University of Paris against the Mendicants. As a result, they were allowed to continue to teach, as long as they pledged to be careful not to provoke the rest of the clergy and to exert caution and wisdom in their argument in favour of "Evangelical Poverty". This relaxed the tension slightly, even though the Franciscans remained suspicious of the university authorities. What made the situation more sensitive for the Franciscans was that many of them, following what they believed to be the example of Francis of Assisi, denigrated theological study.

In this context, Bonaventure's position within the Franciscan order can be surprising. Not only did he study theology, but he was one of the greatest minds of the age, along with Thomas Aquinas. Moreover, Bonaventure was at the cutting edge of theological thinking through his appropriation of Aristotle's philosophy. While he did not do so to the degree that Thomas Aquinas had, and while he did not hesitate to criticise the weaknesses of Aristotelian thinking, that did not prevent him from quoting the Greek philosopher extensively. He was legitimately concerned about unwise applications of Aristotle's philosophy in theological investigation, but he was wise enough to recognise the positive use of Aristotelian categories.

In theological formulation and creativity, Bonaventure was more a "traditionalist" than Thomas Aquinas. He had a natural tendency to follow accepted opinions, though he reworded them, giving new life to theological truths. However, this should not lead us to think he was merely restating what others had already written. His theological explanations could be really original and imaginative, though he took great care never to move away from what he considered to have come from Augustine—the great Father of the Church.

Among the differences between these two great minds, Bonaventure's "mysticism" stands out. In Bonaventure, there is a sense of God's continuous presence. It permeates all of his writings, as well as his life's work. This ordinary presence of God has led some to call him a mystic, though this term is always difficult to define. The fact remains: the best example of medieval mysticism in the thirteenth century is without doubt

Bonaventure's *The Soul's Journey into God*. For him, God's presence nourished a profound devotion, which was an essential part of theological knowledge. Knowledge included devotion, but also wisdom. To him devotion and wisdom were not merely a practical application of theological knowledge. Even in theological thinking, wisdom is always present. God's wisdom permeates every action and every thought.

This explains why we find in Bonaventure a great synthesis of theological investigation and spiritual affections. The results are works which are much less analytical in outlook compared to those of Thomas Aquinas. Bonaventure's treatises bear the mark of someone who was drawn to a more synthetical approach to theology. To Bonaventure, going back to his theological predecessors was not only a mark of humility, but also of wisdom. He was trying to infuse all his thinking with the biblical knowledge inherited from Augustine, and so transformed, or rather translated Patristic theology for a new age. Bonaventure's reverence for the depth and beauty of Scripture did not deter him from seeking wisdom in the theology of his predecessors.

Mysticism and wisdom constitute the two main components of Bonaventure's Christian life. His great defence of a life of poverty will remain one of the great works in this controversy. For Bonaventure, the life of poverty, as a sign of true discipleship, was not mere legalistic observance. It was also the consequence of love of God and applied wisdom.

Bonaventure and Christian wisdom

For Bonaventure, Christian wisdom was the essential outward manifestation of the true knowledge of God: it was key to the journey leading to God. Wisdom should be our daily orientation. That is why we should tend towards wisdom, though Bonaventure never promotes wisdom for its own sake. The fundamental conviction that led Bonaventure to this conclusion is his conviction that reality consisted of two "books".

The first one is the perceptible and natural world: the Book of Nature. Because God is the creator of all things, including all spheres and activities of human life, there was a seed of God's wisdom in every field of human knowledge, not only in the knowledge of God. This means that only wisdom could bring unity to the Christian and human life. It is the uniting virtue of all we are and do. The second one is the eternal Word of God: wisdom itself. It is the Word of God who brings all back to God by the work of redemption.

The imparting of wisdom was necessary because it was essential to knowledge. In fact, without wisdom, humans cannot know anything. They would be like illiterate men trying to read a book. This means that, for Bonaventure, wisdom is the condition of knowledge. There can be no true knowledge without wisdom. For Bonaventure that conviction was not pragmatic, it was founded in God. It is God who is the giver of knowledge, and in Him a knowledge and wisdom coexist in their entirety. God's knowledge is His wisdom, and His wisdom is knowledge. If God's mark has been left by the creator on His creation, knowledge of created things must be knowledge of wisdom.

The implication is radical: for Bonaventure wisdom was a true quality of the Christian. It was the vital character of the Christian life. Wisdom is the virtue that God's Spirit will infuse in the soul until this gift transforms every moment. Christians must be wholly dependent on the life of the Spirit if they are to attain wisdom on the journey to God. By themselves, they cannot reach that goal. God's transformative power is necessary because the finite (human knowledge) is incapable of knowing and comprehending God, the infinite. It is God's grace that draws the finite human soul towards Himself and He who gives wisdom.

Knowledge and wisdom are thus a consequence of grace. For Bonaventure, wisdom can at times look "natural", and be found in all fields of human activity. This explains why all people can demonstrate a degree of wisdom. True and complete wisdom, however, is only possible when the soul finds the place where it can be at rest. This place is where knowledge of God and wisdom in the Christian life embrace each other. This is only possible when we find our rest in God, who embraces all human knowledge. The infinite truth and goodness that is God, manifested outwardly in His wisdom, is the ultimate end of all knowledge.

There is a profound lesson for us. Sometimes theologians give the impression that theology is a purely intellectual exercise, and that knowing God is only possible for the academically trained. Nothing can be further from the truth. Theology is what we do as soon as we talk about God, read the Scriptures, and pray. We are all theologians, as soon as we open the Bible. Pastors and theologians can also act and talk as if wisdom was only for a trained elite. What yields wisdom is fear of God, and studying His Word.

Of course, this view of wisdom would not be complete without another virtue: love. Bonaventure is too astute and too biblical a theologian not to know that love is the cardinal virtue. "As for prophecies, they will pass away; as for tongues, they will cease; as for knowledge, it will pass away" (1 Cor. 13:8). Love, however, will endure forever. Wisdom and love are mutually indispensable. This has wonderful implications because it encourages us to embrace knowledge, i.e. wisdom and love, as being intimately related.

While this is a great insight, Bonaventure's most profound observation about wisdom is that it is founded on one essential principle. He was convinced that the Word of God was the agent of creation and as a result the Word is truly the origin and example for everything. Wisdom, whether philosophical or applied, was nothing other than the knowledge of God's Word. For Bonaventure, wisdom is never separated from God's Word. And so, it is never separated from the person of Christ, the true incarnate Word of God.

In Him, love and wisdom are manifest to their fullest, because He is the Word. He is God's wisdom personified in Proverbs 1-9. Christ, who demonstrated God's love towards mankind, is both the power (Rom. 1:16) and the wisdom of God (1 Cor. 1:30). For Bonaventure, this meant that Christ was the door to all human knowledge. Through Christ, the wisdom of God, we can find the interpretation of all human knowledge. Here, we find Bonaventure's mysticism at work: God the creator speaks, and He is heard in nature and Scripture; Christ is the Word and wisdom of God, and we are remade in His image by the Spirit; thus Christ is the key to embodying wisdom in all fields of true human knowledge.

This Christological focus explains why Bonaventure founded wisdom on God as the God who speaks. Wisdom can be our virtue, because God has spoken in His Word. God communicates, that is a key quality of His nature. He is, in Himself, a self-communicative being. If the world is intelligible, it is because God communicates. The communicative nature of mankind is the creaturely image of the communication within the Godhead. The triune God, existing in fellowship of three persons, communicates. The mere fact of human communication and language points to the nature of God, who is Father, Son, and Spirit. Communication is the wonderful work of God, and God always communicates in wisdom. If we can live out wisdom, it is because God communicates and transforms.

Conclusion

For Bonaventure, at the heart of true human wisdom is God's self-communication and presence in all things. This is a lesson we should take to heart. Knowledge should never be purely formal or intellectual, neither should it be directed first at economics and performance. Because it reflects the existence of the God who speaks in the books of nature and in Scripture, knowledge is always directed towards God. Because God—given for us in Christ, God the Son—is wisdom, our knowledge should always be directed, and motivated by wisdom towards God. God is all for us, and His Word is His own communication.

God speaks: that was one of the keys to Bonaventure's virtue of wisdom. We are called to demonstrate wisdom in our Christian lives. Bonaventure reminds us, in a very Paulinian manner, that our wisdom should be founded on Christ, the Word of God. As Paul writes, Christ is "the power of God and the wisdom of God" (1 Cor. 1:24), and so God the Father gives us wisdom in Christ, in the same manner that He gives us every other gift.

We will need to exercise this wisdom in all our spheres of activity, not only in our Christian life. How should we find and apply God's wisdom in our daily tasks? Bonaventure instructs us to rely always on His revealed Word. This should guide us and encourage us. God has always spoken to reveal the wisdom of His will, and He continues to do so in Scripture. We do not have to find God's wisdom through an online course on "personal development", or by acquiring a degree in philosophy. To grow in wisdom, we must rely on God having revealed Himself as creator and redeemer in the words of Scripture. This conviction should nourish our faith and devotion, until we grow into the full stature of wisdom who was Christ, the Word of God. Knowledge of God's revelation will instil true wisdom in our souls, minds, and attitudes through the work of the Spirit.

Bonaventure presented wisdom as an essential dimension of the Christian life, first and foremost because he tried to follow the teaching of Scripture. His high view of the authority of God's revealed words led him to see the eternal Word of God, the principle of wisdom itself. In other words, if Bonaventure tried to go back to the Scriptures, it is because of his high view of the Word of God, the second person of the Trinity.

John Wycliffe (1320-1384)

Translator of the Bible

Biographical sketch

No list of those who sought to hold the light of the Gospel aloft in the Middle Ages would be complete without acknowledging John Wycliffe, often referred to as the "Morning Star of the Reformation."

The precise year of Wycliffe's birth is not known but was probably between 1320 and 1324. His early education appears to have been undertaken near his place of birth in Yorkshire. From there he went to study in Oxford around the age of 16, which would have been fairly typical in those times. On completion of his arts degree he was admitted as a junior fellow to Merton College and later as Master of Balliol College, though his tenure was short-lived due to serving a congregation in Lincolnshire around 140 miles away.

It is testimony to the humble spirit of this godly man that though fully at home in the academic context of Oxford he gave himself to the interests of serving his parish—first in Fillingham and later in Lutterworth with which he is so closely associated. He was appointed to the latter by the crown, the King himself being an admirer due to Wycliffe's defense of the King's position in regard to a dispute with the pope over the payment of tribute.

Wycliffe hardly endeared himself to the ecclesiastical authorities by denouncing the pope as the antichrist; "the proud worldly priest of Rome". Theologically, he attacked the doctrine of transubstantiation. Pastorally, he translated the Scriptures from Latin into the vernacular and organised itinerant preachers who became known as Lollards to preach the Gospel in the English countryside. This did nothing to enhance his reputation in Rome. After his death, not only were his opinions condemned, but his body was dug up, burned, and the ashes cast on the River Avon.

Socio-political context

It is always necessary to examine the lives of historical figures in the context of the age in which they lived and to recognise that none lived isolated from significant events affecting the wider community. For Wycliffe these included The Babylonian Captivity (1309-1376), The Hundred Years War (1337-1453), and the Black Death which reached its peak in 1348. Each of these had an impact on Wycliffe and help us to understand the matters that occupied his thinking and informed his response. The ebb and flow of international politics will also help explain how he managed to avoid martyrdom—even if his body was ultimately exhumed, his remains burned, and then scattered on the river.

Not for the first time in our examination of the passing of the centuries, the much-vexed relationship between church and state had a significant part to play. The early centuries were marked by bloody martyrdoms of the saints until the conversion of Constantine brought more than relief. The previously despised followers of The Way gained not only social acceptability but even a degree of preference in Imperial Rome. When Constantine moved his capital to Constantinople, the pope, whether it was his desire or not, became *de facto* "First Citizen". Consequently, it fell to pope Leo I to meet face-to-face with Attila the Hun when he threatened Rome. The fact that he made it back alive and was credited with turning the rampaging horde away from the gates greatly enhanced papal authority. As Islam rose and conquered a considerable part of the Eastern Empire, some of the old centres of Christianity were, if not expunged, reduced in their significance. Only the pope in Rome and the Patriarchate in Constantinople were left on the Christian stage. Rome boasted connection with Peter and Paul whereas Constantinople's claim was simply that they were close to the political centre of power. Nor should the gulf between language and culture be underestimated. The citizens in Constantinople may have thought of themselves as Romans but the last emperor to speak Latin was Justinian at the end of the sixth century. The fissure caused by the Great Schism between East and West in 1054 was surprising not so much in that it happened, as that it did not occur sooner.

At the opening of the second millennium Christendom was divided. Eastern Orthodoxy had the Emperor on side and the trajectory of the church/state relationship traced a different path to that of Western Catholicism. Of course, there were political authorities that needed to be reckoned with but none with the legacy of a Roman Emperor. When Pepin granted the Papal States to the pope, the one who sat in the chair of Peter also gained a royal throne. At the Christmas Day service in A.D. 800 in Rome, attended by Pepin's son, Charlemagne, the pope placed a crown on his head and styled him "Holy Roman Emperor". This may or may not have been with the encouragement of Charlemagne. Ecclesiastical records wish to present the event as the Church investing Charlemagne with the authority to rule, but the court chroniclers leave one with the impression that Charlemagne was far from pleased, desiring to be known for having accomplished his position by his own abilities and force of arms rather than receiving it lamely from the hand of the pope. The question of who had authority to do what, and over whom, continued to play into the interactions of church and state; there was a major outbreak of hostility in 1077 between Gregory VII and Henry IV.

By the time we get to the early fourteenth century papal thinking had crystallised into the most significant document of the relationship between Church and State in the medieval period. It was called *Unam Sanctam* and was a papal bull penned by Boniface VIII in 1302. By that time the pope in Rome had exercised considerable political influence as effectively "first citizen" for over a thousand years. He was also a significant political figure in his own right and had been for 500 years. At the beginning of the fourteenth century the pope sought to make explicit what had been implicit, at least in the papal mind, for centuries: whenever there was a clash between royal and papal authority, the former must yield to the latter. The position was clear that as Christ's representative on earth, and as Christ is the King of kings, then the pope was the one who exercised ultimate authority not only in matters ecclesiastical, but in the broader political sphere also. The pope declared that he had authority to sanction, and ultimately to depose kings from their throne. Ecclesiastical authority had come a long way from the days of Constantine!

Of course, kings did not receive this well. Pope Boniface VIII had spent much of his earlier career abroad in diplomatic service which may have given him a taste for involvement, if not actual interference, with the politics of the nations of Europe. He was inevitably on a collision course with a king and the King of France, Philip IV, was happy to step into that role. Those in ultimate political authority, whatever form that takes, seem always hungry for more resources as Samuel warned the children of Israel when they desired to have a king to rule over them. On this occasion the king of France wanted to tax the clergy at the rate of 50 percent. Boniface responded by instructing the church in France to refuse to pay. Philip sent an army to deal with the troublesome cleric. Though the accounts of the meeting between the leader of the French Army, Nogaret, and the pope are not conclusive, it would appear that at the very least the French commander slapped the 73-year-old pope across the face or may even have had him beaten. For his part, the pope excommunicated the King. Whatever the case, the pope was held in custody and died a month later.

His successor, Benedict XI, was sympathetic to France, lifting the excommunication of King Philip his predecessor had imposed. However, Benedict had Nogaret excommunicated for his part in the death of his predecessor and when Benedict died only eight months later this inevitably gave rise to the rumour of his having been poisoned by Nogaret.

It was clear that having someone to succeed Benedict XI who was entirely sympathetic to the French king would be a wonderful asset. He found just such a person in Raymond Bertrand de Got of Aquitaine. He let it be known that were he crowned pope, King Philip would find in him an ally. Raymond found himself duly appointed as pope Clement V. He did not, however, move to Rome but to Avignon for what became known as the Babylonian Captivity, or Avignon Papacy, lasting around seventy years. It was during this period that Philip, having borrowed large sums from the Knights Templar, sought their suppression (and coincidentally the cancellation of his debt). Clement V gave his approval. It may be that Clement was simply in the pocket of Philip or that yielding to the inevitable outcome, he did not wish the prestige of the Papal See to suffer loss by being powerless, or even to inhibit the direction in which the King of France was heading.

By the time the Hundred Years' War began in 1337, the Papacy had spent close to thirty years in Avignon and was in no position to challenge the French king. Inevitably the pope in Avignon sided with the King in Paris against the King of England. Wycliffe would only have been a young lad at the time but old enough to know the pope stood in opposition to his native land, endearing himself to neither ruler nor ruled. But greater troubles lay ahead.

The Papal court in Avignon was not one to hold back on extravagant expenditure and enjoyed the very finest of fare. There was perhaps something of a hint of the "health and wealth" message and that this was a demonstration that the pope was the recipient of God's favour. That might seem plausible in a time of plenty but difficult to maintain when the Black Death came to Europe, wiping out somewhere between 25 and 60 per cent of the population. If sumptuous banquets were a sign of God's blessing, then what was one to make of the worst plague ever to afflict mankind?

The death toll resulting from the Plague was greatly increased by so many of the population moving to cities. As in China, and throughout the history of nations, people have moved towards major urban areas in search of work or just a means of putting food on the table for themselves and their families. Poor sanitation and proximity of accommodation greatly accelerated the advance of the Plague. Yet there was a benefit to the urbanisation of the population. Education among the lower strata of society and those wanting to better themselves increased and the general level of literacy improved. The social pressures inevitably would give rise to great upheavals. With half the population suddenly removed, those who were left found their labour much in demand, but those paying their wages were not willing to recognise that it was "not business as usual" once the Plague had spent its fury. When that is combined with increased education and literacy, the stage was set for conflict between the competing strata. In England this came in the Wat Tyler rebellion of 1381. Though it was ultimately suppressed, the world, at least society in England, would never return to the serfdom of pre-Plague feudalism.

The nature of the Church's authority

This was the world in which Wycliffe moved, and an understanding of the social and political—not to forget of course the ecclesiastical—setting is essential for an appreciation of his contributions and what prompted them.

Pope Boniface VIII, following the trajectory of papal history for centuries, had declared that the ultimate authority in the world was the pope himself. And yet the popes in Avignon were clearly dominated by the King of France and seemed incapable of independent thought or action. If the pope could be held captive and was seemingly little more than a bird in a gilded cage then what of his supreme authority, and how should those who were not aligned with his custodian (or was it jailer?) view his edicts? Even more fundamental was the question of epistemology: how we know what we know. Was the pope the supreme authority because as supreme authority he had declared himself so to be, or was there some other basis on which his authority rested, and if so what was that authority?

We have already seen with men such as Bernard of Clairvaux a desire to look to Scripture as the source of authority. It is highly significant that in his writings he quotes Scripture multiple times on each page but does not seek to confirm his theology by reference to the pope. That heavy dependence on God's Word was undoubtedly the reason that both Luther and Calvin held him in such high esteem. Later Peter Waldo commissioned those with the skills to translate books of the Bible into the language used every day by ordinary people. Wycliffe continued in this same tradition which he was well equipped to do as one with knowledge of the ancient languages. It is thought that he personally translated the New Testament into the English of his day while his students translated the Old Testament under his supervision. The purpose was clear. The consequences were no less so.

Wycliffe wanted ordinary folk, in a day in which more and more were becoming literate, to be able to read the Bible for themselves and draw their own conclusions. Later William Tyndale would say his great objective was for the boy attending the plough to know his Bible as well as the village priest—if not better. For his boldness he was burnt at the stake. William Tyndale was but following the course mapped out for him by Wycliffe. So why was Wycliffe not burnt at the stake? In God's providence, He raised up Wycliffe at a time when the King of England was receptive to the perspective that the pope was not the ultimate authority over kings. Wycliffe, as he relied on the

Scripture, wrote *De Civili Dominio*. This was a direct challenge to the authority the pope claimed in *Unam Sanctam*. However, it came at a time when the pope was aligned with England's ancient foe, France. Wycliffe held that even the pope was subject to the Bible. The result was that powerful political figures were able to protect him against the inevitable backlash. When Wycliffe was summoned for trial to Lambeth Palace, the residence of the Archbishop of Canterbury just across the River Thames from Westminster, the centre of political power in England, he was able to attend with some significant political figures and avoided the usual fate of those who challenged ecclesiastical authority.

The following year he wrote concerning the Eucharist. There is a tendency to suppose that the doctrines currently espoused by the Church of Rome have been held from the beginning— with the possible exception of the New Testament period. It is certainly what our Roman Catholic friends would have us believe. It may come as a surprise that such a central doctrine as "transubstantiation" was not officially adopted until the Fourth Lateran Council of 1215, or to put it a different way, the doctrine had only been adopted the previous century. As Wycliffe gave consideration to the doctrine in the light of what the Word of God was saying, he concluded that declaring that the bread and wine became the body and blood of Christ was not taught by Scripture.

If the mass did not include the re-sacrificing of Christ then there was no need for a priest. Wycliffe's challenge to the authority of the Church was not only to the position of the pope but even down at the grass roots level regarding the role of the local priest. Wycliffe's challenge went even further: he sent out preachers with Scriptures in the common tongue to tell them the Good News that is Christ Jesus. By contrast, the Church of Rome reserved to itself the sole right to interpret Scripture. Wycliff sent out itinerant preachers, known as Lollards, who went from town to town and village with their message at a point in the history of the land when literacy had never been higher, and with copies of the written word to consult.

The very nature of Wycliffe and the Lollard preachers was not that of an organised movement, so it was not until more than ten years after his death that anything approaching a statement of their position was set down. This came in the form of Twelve Conclusions published in 1395.

It began by dealing with the state of the church. Before the Plague struck, the popes had seen their lives of luxury as proof of God's blessing. The response in the face of the Black Death was to issue a plenary indulgence. Those who had died from the bubonic plague went to heaven without the need for a time in purgatory. If that sounds rather convenient in our day, it might have sounded much the same then. The Lollards had a different understanding. The plague was the judgement of God on the corruption of the church: faith, hope and charity had fled and been replaced by pride. From their attack on the Church as a whole the Lollards moved to the priesthood. As they read Scripture they did not see the ministry as then exemplified by the priesthood. It is interesting the way in which the writers argue: "This conclusion is proved: for the priesthood of Rome is made with signs, rites, and bishops' blessings, and that is of little virtue. Nowhere ensampled in the Holy Scripture, for the bishops ordinals in the New Testament be little of record. That the celibacy of the clergy had given rise to sodomy."

In the fourth conclusion they state explicitly their opposition to transubstantiation: "the sacrament of bread induces all men but a few to idolatry, for they ween that Christ's body, that never shall out of heaven, by virtue of the priest's word should be essentially enclosed in a little bread, that they show to the people".

In the following "conclusion" they speak against exorcisms and hallowing. According to the Lollards this has more in common with necromancy than with holy theology.

117

In the sixth "conclusion," the Lollards express their concern for the way in which those who hold office in the Church might also hold office in the state. Such persons are likened to hermaphrodites. It is the Lollards' desire that Parliament should excuse all curates high and low from their temporal office so that they might attend to the cure of souls placed in their charge.

In the next "conclusion" they go so far as to say that they mightily affirm their opposition to prayers for the dead. They offer two reasons. The first is that prayers should be made out of Christian charity, and the second is that it is offensive to God to pray for those who are under God's judgement. This may not be quite what we are hoping for and yet nevertheless their feet are on the path that lead to the church door at Wittenberg.

Then follows their conclusions in regard to pilgrimages, confession and supposed absolution, an attack on granting plenary indulgences for those who take part in a Crusade, female vows of continence which end in "the most horrible sin" of abortion, and finally arts and crafts which the Lollards held to be unnecessary in the New Testament age as we should be satisfied with bodily food and clothing without the need for goldsmiths or silversmiths.

From the list it can be seen that they were not concerned with framing a detailed theology. What they did write was nonetheless a clear challenge to ecclesiastical authority.

Conclusion

We noted at the beginning of the chapter that John Wycliffe is described as the "Morning Star" of the Reformation. This may be misleading. If all that is meant by the term is that he was a reforming influence before the time of Luther and Calvin then it would pass without comment. If, however, the intention is to convey that all was dark before his arrival on the scene then it would not be accurate. Wycliffe had a high view of Scripture and sought to decide theological matters by an appeal to the

John Wycliffe (1320–1384)

Word of God alone. But he was not the first. This was clearly the intent of Bernard of Clairvaux. He eagerly sought to place copies of the Bible in the hands of ordinary folk in the language that they spoke every day. But Wycliffe had a keen desire to send out his followers with the message of the Gospel. But he was not the first to do so. Peter Waldo was doing much the same long before Wycliffe was born. Indeed, after his death many would be burned for their activities.

None of this is to undervalue the work of Wycliffe much less to denigrate his contribution. Rather it is to demonstrate that Wycliffe held aloft the light of the Gospel in his generation as others had done before him.

Jan Hus (1372-1415)

From Goose to Eagle

With Jan Hus we arrive at the very brink of the Reformation, and some of the disparate strands come together. Bernard of Clairvaux always emphasised the use of Scripture in his writings and earned the admiration of Luther and Calvin. Peter Waldo saw the importance of declaring the truth of the Gospel through the use of Scripture. For this he and his followers were persecuted. Though the Waldensian movement was French in its origins, the descendants of the itinerant preachers under persecution fled first to the mountains of northern Italy for safety and then to other parts of Europe. One area which received communities of Waldensians was Bohemia around the capital, Prague. This, then, was fertile ground for communities with a high view of Scripture and a tradition of preaching based on the Word of God.

Biographical sketch

Jan Hus, whose last name meant "goose", was born into a family that, though not impoverished, was not particularly wealthy and lived in a rural part of Bohemia. He was obviously a young man of considerable intellectual ability, and early on decided that the priesthood would be a suitable outlet for his gifts. It was not that he had a deep sense of calling, but that he sought the promise of a comfortable living. It was thus that he headed for the University of Prague which had been founded comparatively recently—just a few decades before in 1348. Though the university was situated in Prague, the overwhelming majority of the faculty was German, which was also true of the student body. This was no doubt caused in part by the domination of the German states in politics, but part of the explanation also lies in the fact that the lands further westward had benefitted from being under the influence of the Roman Empire. One corollary of this was that German had acquired an alphabet before the nations further east. This in turn meant that there was a capacity to record and pass on information from one generation to another. The written texts of generations were available as a ready resource to be called on. The setting down of the languages of the nations and tribes further east came much later, so Czech people did not have the same wealth of learning on which to draw. That is not to say that those who were Czech did not aspire to equal their German-speaking colleagues.

This was the Prague to which Hus arrived at to study at the university. He probably matriculated around 1390 but by 1401 had been appointed Dean of the Philosophy Department. It was during this time that he became interested in the works of Wycliffe, and was swift to acknowledge the influence in his thinking. He was appointed the preacher in the Bethlehem Chapel in Prague and quickly made a name for himself as an outstanding Czech Bible expositor. The seeds he was casting fell on fertile soil with at least some of the hearers coming from Waldensian stock used to having the word read and proclaimed to them in their own language. Just as Wycliffe desired the ordinary people to have God's word available to them in their own language, so likewise Hus sought to preach and speak to them in the vernacular. Add to this that, at last, there seemed to be a prominent Czech as opposed to German speaker, it might seem inevitable that his popularity soared.

Socio-political and theological context

Before we can examine the life of Jan Hus in greater detail we need first of all to look at the context in which he lived.

In the previous chapter it became apparent that moving the papacy from Rome to Avignon meant that the French King was able to control the pope. In the seventy years of the "Babylonian Captivity of the Church" the papacy suffered a significant drop in prestige as its independence was critically compromised. But worse was still to come. Gregory XI was the seventh of the Avignon popes and he returned the papacy to Rome in 1377 and died the next year, necessitating the election of a successor. There was inevitable pressure for an Italian to be elected as had been so often the custom until the time of the Avignon Papacy. It will come as no surprise that the King of France had ensured that those appointed as Peter's successor should be French. Gregory XI was in fact the last Frenchman to be recognised as pope though not the last to claim the title.

The cardinals met in conclave but did not appear to be arriving at a conclusion speedily enough for the Roman mob. They burst into the assembly and insisted on the election of an Italian pope there and then. The cardinals, fearing for their lives with some justification, obliged the mob. Thereafter, the French cardinals withdrew back to Avignon where they set about electing another pope and denouncing the one appointed under duress. There was thus a pope in Rome and a pope in Avignon. The one in Avignon unsurprisingly had the support of the King of France and those nations, states or cities with which he was allied. Those such as England, which was still engaged in what would become known as the Hundred Years' War, inevitably aligned with the pope in Rome. This was known as the Papal Schism and lasted from the death of Gregory XI in 1378 until a resolution was put in place at the Council of Constance in 1415. It was, of course, a huge scandal that there were two popes, each excommunicating the other in the fiercest of terms.

It was not just that each pope maintained his own legitimacy, perhaps the even greater problem was how to resolve the conflict. Given that the popes had accrued considerable authority to the point that the official position was that the pope was God's representative on earth, and as such ruled over kings, or at least claimed to do so, the problem was—to whom was a pope accountable? Who could make the judgement that one pope was legitimate and another was an anti-pope? By definition, there was no one who had such authority. It was out of these circumstances that what became known as the Conciliar Movement arose. The desire was obvious and one shared by the whole of Christendom, that the situation of having two competing popes should be brought to an end. To accomplish this a Council met in Pisa in 1409. Its decision was to depose both popes and appoint a third. Though it seemed quite rational, the problem was that neither of the existing popes recognised the authority of the Council, and the net result was that there were now three popes in Christendom. If having two popes was a reproach on Christendom then adding a third was certainly not an improvement.

Jan Hus' life and influence

It was into the ecclesiastical turmoil of the Papal Schism that Jan Hus was born. Being born around 1372 would have made him around six when Gregory XI returned the papacy to Rome and died shortly thereafter. Effectively, Hus' life coincided with the Papal Schism which was brought to an end at the same time as his life was brought to an end. The two were not unrelated.

But it was not the theology of those who held office that Hus preached, but the authority and inspiration of God's word, especially in the Gospels. His teaching was first condemned by the Archbishop of Prague. But still he continued to preach in the Bethlehem Chapel. His teaching was also condemned by pope John XXIII—one of the three popes there were at that time. Pope John was no paragon of virtue. Edward Gibbon in *Decline and Fall of the Roman Empire* declared sardonically that ultimately he was charged and found guilty of piracy, rape, sodomy, murder, and incest after the more scandalous charges were suppressed.

Like Luther a hundred years later, Hus was deeply troubled by the sale of indulgences. The Church argued that it had the authority to release souls languishing in purgatory and send them straight to Heaven. The Church had supposedly used that power in granting full plenary absolution to those going on Crusade and, at the time of the Black Death, to those who died. Hus argued that if the Church did indeed have such authority, then Christian charity would dictate that it should use it for all and do so immediately. Why would the Church not ease the sufferings of the saints when she had the power to do so? If she were to release without financial gain the souls of those in purgatory she would lose a notable source of income. Was that the real reason she did not use her authority to release souls from purgatory? Luther used this argument a hundred years later in his famous 95 Theses. Attacking abstruse points of theology was one thing but undermining a revenue stream was another! It led to greater persecution and Hus being excommunicated a second time. The pope summoned him to appear, but which pope was the one rightfully to be obeyed? The University of Prague maintained a position of neutrality. It is an indication of how the Papal Schism undermined the papal authority.

Hus continued to preach and to write. In 1412 he published *De Ecclesia*. This was more a manifesto than a work of theology. In it he affirms such doctrines as Christ being the head of the Church and not the pope, the infallibility of Scripture and the fallibility of the pope, the abuse of Scripture in the pursuit of clerical power, that only the one sinned against could forgive a sin, undermining the power of the priest to grant absolution, the rejection of blind obedience, and that ecclesiastical superiors are not always to be obeyed. There were twenty-three chapters in all, and they were a very clear challenge to church authorities from the pope down. In affirming that the laity should receive the cup as well as the bread he was making a simple statement which won immediate widespread appeal. The argument for receiving both elements in communion was simple and at the same time undermined the division between ordinary members of the church and the priesthood. Only the latter were permitted to receive the wine. The priesthood was on a different level to the generality of the faithful.

Hus was certainly an irritant to ecclesiastical authority, but geo-politically the far more fundamental problem was about who could rightfully claim the title of pope. In the meantime, Hus could legitimately claim that he did not know which pope had to be obeyed. No one did! Or at least, everyone had their own opinion which amounted to the same thing.

Though the Conciliar Movement had made an attempt in 1409 to resolve the most vexing issue in Christendom, it had only succeeded in muddying the waters by adding a third pope. A further attempt was made by calling for a church council in Constance in 1414. Hus was summoned but initially declined until the Holy Roman Emperor, Sigismund, offered safe conduct and an armed guard to protect him. Under those conditions, Hus accepted—no doubt with the hope that he would be given an opportunity to argue his position. He did not read the fine print however. The safe conduct was to bring him to the Council, and no safe conduct was guaranteed for his return. As soon as Hus entered the town, those who had been his guardians became his jailers. He was arrested and thrown into a dungeon which was as dark and miserable as the name implies. For eight months Hus was kept in dark and dank surroundings with vermin his companions and a little food—and that only of the lowest quality. His health was broken but not his spirits.

In the meantime, the members of the Council set about reducing the number of popes from three down to one. Pope John XXIII was deposed as a result of the long list of crimes of which he stood accused. It is worthwhile noting that he was never defrocked and he lived out his days in the comfort of one holding the office of Cardinal. Jan Hus, however, was not to get off so lightly. After eight months in a dungeon he was brought before the Council and asked to recant. No opportunity was afforded him to defend his opinions. For the Council this was a minor matter of business that needed to be decided quickly so they could get back to the main agenda. As with Luther a century later, Hus stood his ground. The next day he was taken out and burned at the stake. There were thus two Johns who were tried before the Council of Constance. There was John XXIII who was accused of piracy, rape, sodomy, murder, and incest but was simply demoted to Cardinal and lived out the rest of his life in comfort, and there was [John] Jan Hus who was accused of teaching doctrines that were contrary to the Church, who was not allowed to defend himself and was summarily executed by being burnt to death. This was not the Church's finest hour.

Jan Hus was translated from this world into the world to come with courage and firmness of mind. He even punned on his own name that though the authorities were burning a goose, God would cause an eagle to rise. A century later Martin Luther stood accused of being a Husite. He did not hesitate to be identified with one who had given his life to uphold the authority of God's word. There may be another way in which Luther benefitted from the martyrdom of Hus. Sigismund was excoriated for giving a safe conduct to Hus and then allowing him to be burned at the stake without even the opportunity of defending himself. This was, and remains, a black mark against him. Charles V was called upon to give the most prominent Husite of his day safe conduct. He kept his word and allowed Luther to depart in peace. Did the opprobrium heaped on Sigismund affect the decision of Charles V? Perhaps. We cannot say that for certain but the pressure would be in the right direction, and Luther was kept safe.

Conclusion

We have now arrived at the very eve of the Reformation. Luther did not burst upon the scene with no connection to the past. He was accused of being a Husite—and though Jan Hus was burned at the stake as a heretic, Luther did not hesitate to align himself with him. But Hus was not the originator of the doctrines he taught. He drew heavily and openly upon the works of Wycliffe and the Waldensians even though those works had been formally condemned by the pope, who ordered Wycliffe's remains to be dug up, burned, and the ashes scattered on the river. Wycliffe himself was not the originator of a high view of Scripture, or of making the Word of God available to ordinary people. Before the Lollards were going from town to town and from village to village in England, the followers of Waldo were doing much the same in the towns and villages of southern France. When persecution drove Waldensians from their homes, a portion of them made their way to Prague and the surrounding area, providing a ready hearing for Hus and his followers. Far from Luther being a sudden flash of light bursting surprisingly on the scene bringing an end to the so-called "Dark Ages", he was, in fact the beneficiary of those who had gone before. In God's providence he was able to build on the faithful labours of previous generations.

Conclusion

It is now time to close the long centuries of the medieval age. We have journeyed from the frontiers of the early Church to the eve of the Reformation. We have crossed ten centuries in these ten chapters. We have met towering figures of the history of the Church, some well-known, others just emerging from a long obscurity. We hope to have introduced them in a light that has been both instructive and edifying.

The main thrust of this book was that the light of the Gospel was not expunged when Constantine made it acceptable to openly be a part of the Church of Jesus Christ. The King and Head of the Church had his witnesses down through the generations. The doctrines of the Church of Rome may have their proponents from an early generation, but they were only gradually adopted and were often challenged. Neither Protestantism nor what is now known as Catholicism sprang fully clothed and ready for battle as Athena is depicted in ancient Greek mythology. They existed alongside one another and struggled each in turn for wider acceptance.

Though it might run counter to the common perception, the formation of Roman Catholicism might indeed be dated to the Council of Trent, which would make it a more recent theological statement than that of the magisterial Reformers. Those in the Roman tradition would wish you to believe that theirs is the original theology dating back to Peter, and that the Reformation sprang from virtually nowhere in the sixteenth century. Those of us who sit on the other side of the table would wish to return the favour. Though the Council of Trent came to represent the majority of those who retained their allegiance to Rome, Reformers were claiming that their theology was that of the New Testament. In addition they were maintaining and building on those who throughout the intervening centuries had held aloft the Gospel hope.

In these ten chapters, we have tried to explain how throughout the medieval ages we see threads of theological and biblical truths. In so doing, we are not trying to impose our Protestant theology on our medieval forefathers. That would be an easy and, frankly, quite an excusable mistake. It is easy to justify one's position by appealing to the great figures of the past. We all do that very thing, maybe even without noticing it. There is nothing like an appeal to some authority to avoid the hard task of understanding these theologians for what they believed, rather than what we hope they believed.

To avoid this mistake, we have been careful to introduce our authors and their times. We have made our way through times with which we are unfamiliar to reach Luther and Calvin, and the Protestant Reformation of the sixteenth century. What we have witnessed through these long centuries is God's faithfulness towards His Church. He has never left her without faithful witnesses and teachers. While we can often have the impression that there was only a handful of true witnesses of the Gospel in the medieval ages—and sometimes we add "if any!"—the history we have read together paints a different picture, in which, despite their flaws, many medieval theologians were trying to be faithful to God, to hold to a high view of Scripture, and to love Christ and His Church.

These pages encourage us to be humble in the face of God's active providence in history. When we consider our own lives, the way we talk about Christ, the frailty of our Christian life, and our own faults and follies, how could we not humbly recognise that we are no better or more perfect than many of them? Reading these theologians, our fathers in the faith, we are moved towards the triune God. We stop being obsessed with our supposed theological superiority and stand ready to discover more about God's person, presence, and grace.

For further reading:

Davis, R. H. C. *A History of Medieval Europe: From Constantine to Saint Louis.* London: Routledge, 2014.

González, Justo L. *The Story of Christianity: Volume 1: The Early Church to the Dawn of the Reformation.* New York: HarperOne, 2014.

Johnson, Paul. *History of Christianity.* New York: Touchstone, 2014.

Latourette, Kenneth Scott. *A History of the Expansion of Christianity.* Vol. 2: The Thousand Years Of Uncertainty A D 500 A D 1500. New York: Harper, 1938.

Needham, Nick. *2,000 Years of Christ's Power,* vol. 2, The Middles Ages. Fearn: Christian Focus, 2016.

Pelikan, Jaroslav. *A History of the Development of Doctrine.* Vol. 3: Growth of Medieval Theology (600-1300). Chicago: University of Chicago Press, 1978.

Schaff, Philip. *History of the Christian Church.* Vols. 3-6. New Delhi: Christian World Imprints, 2015.

Volz, Carl A. *The Medieval Church: From the Dawn of the Middle Ages to the Eve of the Reformation.* Nashville: Abingdon Press, 1997.

Also available from Christian Focus Publications ...

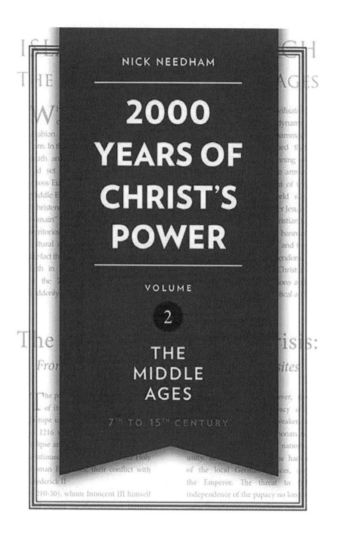

NICK NEEDHAM

2000 YEARS OF CHRIST'S POWER

VOLUME

2

THE MIDDLE AGES

7ᵀᴴ TO 15ᵀᴴ CENTURY

2000 Years of Christ's Power
Vol 2: The Middle Ages
by Nick Needham

The Middle Ages were dubbed the 'Dark Ages' almost before they had begun to draw to a close. Ever since then, they have continued to be seen as a time of hardship and oppression, full of popes and crusades. In the second volume of *2,000 Years of Christ's Power*, another side of the Middle Ages shines through though: The continual workings of Christ as He built His kingdom through figures such as Thomas a Kempis and John Wycliffe, who lived and struggled during these centuries. This was far from a period of stagnation; rather it was the fire from which the Reformation was kindled.

For many years now I have said: if you want a thorough, learned but accessible and well-written history of the church, read Nick Needham's *2,000 Years of Christ's Power*.

Carl R. Trueman, Grove City College, Pennsylvania

Christian Focus Publications

Our mission statement –

STAYING FAITHFUL

In dependence upon God we seek to impact the world through literature faithful to His infallible Word, the Bible. Our aim is to ensure that the Lord Jesus Christ is presented as the only hope to obtain forgiveness of sin, live a useful life and look forward to heaven with Him.

Our books are published in four imprints:

CHRISTIAN FOCUS

Popular works including biographies, commentaries, basic doctrine and Christian living.

CHRISTIAN HERITAGE

Books representing some of the best material from the rich heritage of the church.

MENTOR

Books written at a level suitable for Bible College and seminary students, pastors, and other serious readers. The imprint includes commentaries, doctrinal studies, examination of current issues and church history.

CF4•K

Children's books for quality Bible teaching and for all age groups: Sunday school curriculum, puzzle and activity books; personal and family devotional titles, biographies and inspirational stories – because you are never too young to know Jesus!

Christian Focus Publications Ltd,
Geanies House, Fearn, Ross-shire,
IV20 1TW, Scotland, United Kingdom.
www.christianfocus.com